THE POEMS

of

ST. JOHN OF THE CROSS

THE POEMS
of
ST. JOHN
OF THE CROSS

ORIGINAL SPANISH TEXTS

AND

New English versions

by

John Frederick Nims

Grove Press, Inc.   New York
Evergreen Books Ltd.   London

COPYRIGHT © 1959 BY JOHN FREDERICK NIMS

Library of Congress Catalog Card Number : 58-10844

First Grove Press Edition 1959

Third printing

MANUFACTURED IN THE UNITED STATES OF AMERICA

ACKNOWLEDGMENTS

For the Spanish text of these poems I am grateful to the editorial achievements of the late P. Silverio de Santa Teresa: to his *Cántico espiritual y poesías de San Juan de la Cruz, según el códice de Sanlúcar de Barrameda* (1928) and to his monumental *Obras de San Juan de la Cruz* (1929-31). For permission to present the texts here I am grateful to *Editorial " El Monte Carmelo "* (Burgos) and to the help of its gracious *Administrador*.

The translator wishes to thank the editors of the following magazines for permission to reprint versions which first appeared in their pages: *America, Commonweal, Jubilee, Modern Age, Poetry, Thought, Today*.

DEDICATORIA

A steely morning in this city of swordblades. On the Paseo del Carmen, wind and thrilling height and end of season. The *yo el rey* of foreign jets is fading across heaven; leaves of the linden cry *wir alle fallen*. Here, high above the world, four centuries ago the prince of Spanish poets was thrust in a stone vault: its bars and echoing hollows the true cello of his love.

To see that point in space where wonder struck, I walked, this fittest day of the year, above the gorge of the Tajo, olive-dark and frothing at its crags. Across the canyon, over Roman stone the Saracens rebuilt, the bristling keep of San Servando. Beyond, angry La Sagra—the red country with its groves. This is what he would have seen, given a window in his prison. Or seen briefly had he escaped by daylight instead of pitching from knotted blankets in the dead of night.

His cell? In dizzy air above us. Time and the wars have burst the walls that cramped it, sent them toppling to the torrent or sifting on the wind. His cell: a floating aerie overhead, engraved with sunlight and the fire of stars. To the mind's eye it hovers like a prow from outer space, in rings of radiance. Like luminous flotsam in the skies of Bosch.

Today, no worse intentioned than the friars who jailed and jostled him, I doom his passion to another sort of duress. Another prison, other chains. One hopes for a thin window somewhere, through which at times a glimpse of burning earth, of groves and the jade river; some sliver of his vivid sky; his moonlight once or twice.

J.F.N.

Toledo de Castilla

24 de nov., 1958: el día de San Juan de la Cruz

CONTENTS

II. ADDITIONAL POEMS

III. FROM THE CODEX OF JAÉN

IV. NOTES:

THE POEMS

of

ST. JOHN OF THE CROSS

I

THE CODEX OF
SANLÚCAR
DE BARRAMEDA

CANCIONES ENTRE
el alma y el esposo

Adonde te escondiste
amado y me dexaste con gemido?
como el cieruo huiste
auiendome herido
sali tras ti clamando, y eras ydo.

Pastores los que fuerdes
alla por las majadas al otero
si por uentura vierdes
aquel que yo mas quiero
Dezilde que adolesco, peno, y muero.

Buscando mis amores
yre por esos montes y riberas
ni cogere las flores
ni temere las fieras
y passare los fuertes y fronteras.

pregunta a las
criaturas.

O bosques, y espesuras:
Plantadas por la mano del amado
ô prado de verduras
de flores esmaltado
Dezid si por uosotros ha passado.

respuesta de las
criaturas.

Mil gracias deramando
Passo por estos sotos con presura
e yendolos mirando
con sola su figura
Vestidos los dexo de hermosura.

THE SPIRITUAL CANTICLE
Songs between the soul and the bridegroom

Where have you hidden away?
Never a crumb of comfort day or night,
   Dearest? To wound your prey
   and off like a stag in flight!
I hurried forth imploring you—out of sight!

   The bride

   You shepherds, you that rove
up in the ranches on the mountain's brow,
   if you should meet my love,
   my one love, tell him how
I'm heartsick, fevered, and fast sinking now.

   I'll go myself and scour
highland and lowland over for my dear;
   not dawdle for a flower;
   no fang of prowler fear;
bursting by each confronter and frontier.

   O groves and leafy screen,
foliage planted by a lover's hand,
   meadows of bluegreen
   with marigolds japanned,
tell me, has he been lately in your land?

   A question to
   the creatures

   Lavishing left and right
a world of wonders, he went streaming by
   these orchards, meteor-bright:
   beneath his brilliant eye
rose many a green pavilion to the sky.

   Their response

Esposa.
     Ay quien podra sanarme
acaba de entregarte ya de vero
     no quieras embiarme
     de oy mas ya mensagero
que no saben dezirme lo que quiero.

     I todos quantos vagan
de ti me van mil gracias refiriendo
     y todos mas me llagan
     y dexame muriendo
un no se que que quedan balbuciendo.

     Mas como perseueras
o vida no viuiendo donde viues
     y haziendo porque mueras
     las flechas que reciues
de lo que del amado en ti concibes.

     Porque pues has llagado
aqueste coraçon, no le sanaste?
     y pues me le has robado
     por que assi le dexaste,
y no tomas el robo que robaste?

     Apaga mis enojos
pues que ninguno basta a deshazellos
     y veante mis ojos
     pues eres lumbre dellos
y solo para ti quiero tenellos.

What cure for my disease?   The bride
Give up, give up in earnest. Make an ending.
   These tedious deputies,
    I beg of you, stop sending:
what good are these—pretending and pretending?

   Figures that come and go
bring news of you indeed: what jubilant rumor!
   I reel as with a blow;
    sink stricken at the glimmer
of something heard ecstatic in the stammer.

   Strange! to feel the breath
of life endure, not living where life is.
   Brought low and close to death
    by those bowmen of his—
to each inroad of love sharp witnesses.

   Unready yet to mend
the havoc in this heart—so quick to break it?
   Possess and not intend
    ever to take it?
Have it by force and forceably forsake it?

   Oh shorten the long days
of burning thirst—no other love allays them.
   Let my eyes see your face,
    treasure to daze them.
Except for love, it's labor lost to raise them.

O christalina fuente
si en essos tus semblantes plateados
formases de repente
los ojos desseados
que tengo en mis entrañas dibuxados.

Apartalos amado
que voy de buelo:

bueluete paloma
que el cieruo vulnerado
por el otero asoma
al ayre de tu buelo: y fresco toma.

Mi amado las montañas
los valles solitarios nemorosos
las insulas estrañas
los rios sonorosos
el siluo de los ayres amorosos.

La noche sosegada
En par de los levantes de la aurora
la musica callada
la soledad sonora
la cena que recrea y enamora.

Nuestro lecho florido
de cueuas de leones enlaçado
en purpura tendido
de paz edificado
de mil escudos de oro coronado.

If only, crystal well,
clear in the mirror's silver could arise
　　suddenly by some spell
　　the long awaited eyes
the poor heart scrapes in clay to improvise!

　　Love, cover those bright eyes!
I'm voyaging on air!

　　　　Float downward, dove.　　　　The
　　The stag from covert lies　　　　bridegroom
　　hurt on the hill above,
stirred by your wing he loves the coolness of.

　　My love: the mountain's height;　　The bride
forest ravines and faraway recesses;
　　torrents' sonorous weight;
　　isles no explorer guesses;
the affectionate air all whisper and caresses;

　　the serene flow of night
with dawn a rising twilight in the skies;
　　music of still delight;
　　a desert of sweet cries;
a supper of light hearts and lovelit eyes.

　　Our bed: in roses laid,
patrols of lions ranging all around;
　　of royal purple made,
　　pitched on halcyon ground,
with blazonry of golden bucklers crowned.

A zaga de tu huella
las jouenes discurren al camino
al toque de centella
al adobado vino
emissiones de balsamo diuino.

En la interior bodega
de mi amado beui; y quando salia
por toda aquesta vega
ya cosa no sabia
y el ganado perdi que antes seguia.

Alli me dio su pecho
alli me enseño sciencia muy sabrosa
y yo le di de hecho
a mi sin dexar cosa :
alli le prometi de ser su esposa.

Mi alma se ha empleado
y todo mi caudal en su seruicio
ya no guardo ganado
ni ya tengo otro officio
que ya solo en amar es mi exercicio.

pues ya si en el exido
de oy mas no fuere vista ni hallada
direis que me he perdido
que andando enamorada
me hize perdidiza, y fui ganada.

Breathless, on roads you mark
girls whirl to the four winds; their foreheads shine
   stung by a sudden spark,
   flushed with delightful wine.
What swirls of fragrance widening and divine!

   Shown deeper than before
in cellars of my love I drank; from there
   went wandering on the moor;
   knew nothing, felt no care;
the sheep I tended once are who knows where?

   There he broke secrecy;
had honey of revelation to confide.
   There I gave all of me;
   put chariness aside:
there I promised to become his bride.

   Forever at his door
I gave my heart and soul. My fortune too.
   I've no flock any more,
   no other work in view.
My occupation: love. It's all I do.

   If I'm not seen again
in the old places, on the village ground,
   say of me: lost to men.
   Say I'm adventure-bound
for love's sake. Lost (on purpose) to be found.

De flores y esmeraldas
en las frescas mañanas escogidas
haremos las guirnaldas
en tu amor florecidas
y en un cabello mio entretexidas.

En solo aquel cabello
que en mi cuello bolar consideraste
mirastele en mi cuello
y en el presso quedaste
y en uno de mis ojos te llagaste.

Quando tu me mirauas
tu gracia en mi tus ojos imprimian
por esso me adamauas
y en eso merecian
los mios adorar lo que en ti vian.

No quieras despreciarme
que si color moreno en mi hallaste
ya bien puedes mirarme
despues que me miraste
que gracia y hermosura en mi dexaste.

Cogednos las raposas
que esta ya florecida nuestra viña,
entanto que de rosas
hazemos vna piña
y no paresca nadie en la montiña.

In the cool morning hours
we'll gather many a tender wreath to wear,
with emeralds and dayflowers
sprung in love's summer air.
I'll give for their entwining a lock of hair

curling upon my shoulder—
you loved to see it lifted on the air.
You loved it, fond beholder
caught fascinated there—
my glance embedded then the barb you wear.

Your eyes caressing me
fell on their living image in my own
and loved distractedly.
That stirring look alone
gave mettle to return the fervor shown.

Please, no pitying brow
seeing my cheek was dusky in those days.
Only turn this way now
as once before—that gaze
adorned me fresh and lovely in its rays.

Now that the bloom uncloses
catch us the little foxes by the vine,
as we knit cones of roses
cunning as those of pine.
Let no intruder loom on our skyline.

Detente Cierço muerto
ven austro que recuerdas los amores
aspira por mi huerto
y corran sus olores
y pacera el amado entre las flores.

Esposo.

Entrado se ha la esposa
en el ameno huerto desseado
y a su sabor reposa
el cuello reclinado
sobre los dulces braços de el amado.

Debaxo de el mançano
alli comigo fuiste desposada
alli te di la mano
y fuiste reparada
donde tu madre fuera violada.

A las aues ligeras,
leones, cieruos, gamos saltadores,
montes, valles, riberas,
aguas, ayres, ardores,
y miedos de las noches veladores.

Por las amenas liras,
y canto de serenas os conjuro
que cesen vuestras iras,
y no toqueis al muro
porque la esposa duerma mas seguro.

Dwindle, O wind of death.
Come, southern wind, for lovers; come and stir
   the garden with your breath.
   Make affluent the air.
My love is gladdened among lilies there.

She enters, the bride! closes,
soft, the enchanting garden dreams foretold her.
   Gracefully she reposes;
   my arms enfold her,
her throat affectionate upon my shoulder.

The bridegroom

Under the apple tree
the words of our betrothal and their spell:
   I took you tenderly,
   hurt virgin, made you well
where all the scandal on your mother fell.

Wings twinkling here and there,
lion and gamboling antler, shy gazelle,
   peak, precipice, and shore,
   flame, air, and flooding well,
night-watchman terror, with no good to tell—

by many a pleasant lyre
and song of sirens I command you all:
   bury this wrangling air;
   no nuzzling at the wall.
But let the bride in a deep slumber fall.

Esposa

O nymphas de Judea
entanto que en las flores, y rosales
el ambar perfumea
morâ en los arabales
y no querais tocar nuestros humbrales.

Escondete Carillo
y mira con tu haz a las montañas
y no quieras dezillo
mas mira las campañas
De la que ua por insulas estrañas.

Esposo.

La blanca palomica
al arca con el ramo se a tornado
y ya la tortolica
al socio desseado
en las riberas verdes a hallado.

En soledad biuia
y en soledad a puesto ya su nido
y en soledad la guia
a solas, su querido
tambien en soledad de amor herido.

Esposa

Gozemonos amado
y vamonos a uer en tu hermosura
al monte u al collado
do mana el agua pura
entremos mas adentro en la espesura.

Girls of Jerusalem,   The bride
now that the breath of roses more and more
    eddies on leaf and stem,
    be stranger than before.
Stand further. And no darkening our door.

And darling, settle here.
Look to the mountain ranges; turn your face.
    Hush! nothing in my ear.
    But look what crewmen grace
the passer of fabulous islands in her chase.

The little pearl-white dove   The
with frond of olive to the Ark returns.   bridegroom
    Wedded, the bird of love
    no longer yearns,
nestled above still water, among ferns.

She spent most lonely days,
in loneliest of regions kept her nest,
    her guide on lonesome ways
    her love, who knew them best—
that arrow from the desert in his breast.

A celebration, love!   The bride
Let's revel at both our beauty in your eyes!
    To the hill and heights above!
    cascades that freshen these!
then further, deep and deeper in the trees.

y luego a las subidas
cauernas de la piedra, nos iremos
que estan bien escondidas
y alli nos entraremos
y el mosto de granadas gustaremos.

Alli me mostrarias
aquello que mi alma pretendia
y luego me darias
alli, tu uida mia,
aquello que me diste el otro dia.

El aspirar de el ayre
el canto de la dulce Philomena
el soto y su donayre
en la noche serena
con llama que consume y no da pena.

Que nadie lo miraua
Aminadab tan poco parecia
y el cerco sosegaua
y la caualleria
a uista de las aguas decendia.

And on to the steeple rock
all honeycombed with caverns and with mines
   well off the common track.
   Safe in those high confines
we'll taste the tingle of pomegranate wines.

   There finally you'll show
something my soul long wept and waited for,
   and the same moment, O
   my dearest life, restore
what once upon a time you gave before:

   the breathing of the air,
the nightingale in her affectionate vein,
   woods and the freshness there
   in night's unruffled reign—
these, and the flames embracing without pain.

   None loitering to see:
Aminadab the demon fled affrighted.
   The siege sank quietly.
   The horsemen sighted
vistas of shining water and alighted.

CANCIONES DE

de el alma, que se goza de auer llegado al
alto estado de la perfeccion, que es la
union con Dios por el camino
de la negacion espiritual
De el mesmo
Au-
thor

En una noche obscura
Con ansias en amores inflamada
o dichosa uentura
sali sin ser notada
Estando ya mi casa sosegada

A escuras, y segura
Por la secreta escala disfraçada
o dichosa uentura
a escuras y ençelada
Estando ya mi casa sosegada

En la noche dichosa
En secreto que nadie me ueya.
Ni yo miraua cosa
Sin otra luz y guia
Sino la que en el coraçon ardia

Aquesta me guiaua
Mas cierto que la luz del medio dia
adonde me esperaua
quien yo bien me sabia
En parte donde nadie parecia

THE DARK NIGHT
Songs
of the soul, which rejoices at having reached
that lofty state of perfection:
union with God by the way
of spiritual negation

Once in the dark of night,
my longings caught and raging in love's ray
(O windfall of delight!)
I slipped unseen away
as all my home in a deep slumber lay.

Secure, in more than night,
close hid and up the stair a secret way
(O windfall of delight!)
in the night, in feigned array
as all my home in a deep slumber lay.

There in the lucky dark,
stealing in secrecy, by none espied;
nothing for eyes to mark,
no other light, no guide
but in my heart: that fire would not subside.

That led me on—
that dazzle truer than high noon is true
to where there waited one
I knew—how well I knew!—
in a place where no one was in view.

O noche que guiaste
o noche amable mas que el aluorada
o noche que juntaste
amado con amada
Amada en el amado transformada

En mi pecho florido
que entero para el solo se guardaua
alli quedó dormido,
y yo le regalaua
y el ventalle de cedros ayre daua

El ayre de la almena
quando yo sus cabellos esparzia
con su mano serena
en mi cuello heria
y todos mis sentidos suspendia.

Quedeme y oluideme
El rostro recline sobre el amado
cesò todo, y dexeme
dexando mi cuidado
Entre las açucenas oluidado.

O dark of night, my guide!
O sweeter than anything sunrise can discover!
    O night, drawing side to side
    the loved and lover,
the loved one wholly ensouling in the lover.

    There in my festive breast
walled for his pleasure-garden, his alone,
    the lover remained at rest
    and I gave all I own,
gave all, in air from the cedars softly blown.

    All, in wind from the wall
as my hand in his hair moved lovingly at play.
    He let soft fingers fall
    and I swooned dead away
wounded: all senses in oblivion lay.

    Quite out of self suspended—
my forehead on the lover's own reclined.
    And that way the world ended
    with all my cares untwined
among the lilies falling and out of mind.

CANCIONES DEL

Alma en la intima comunicacion
De union de amor De Dios
del mismo auctor.

O llama de amor uiua
que tiernamente hieres
De mi alma en el mas profundo centro
pues ya no eres esquiua
acaba ya si quieres
Rompe la tela deste dulce enquentro.

O cauterio suaue,
o regalada llaga,
O mano blanda, o toque delicado
que a uida eterna sabe
y toda deuda paga,
matando muerte, en vida la as trocado.

O lamparas de fuego
en cuyos resplandores
las profundas cauernas de el sentido
que estaua oscuro, y ciego
con estraños primores
Calor, y luz dan junto a su querido.

Quan manso, y amoroso
recuerdas en mi seno
Donde secretamente solo moras
y en tu aspirar sabroso
de bien y gloria lleno
quan delicadamente me enamoras.

THE LIVING FLAME OF LOVE
Songs
of the soul in its intimate communion
of union with God's love

O living flame of love!
how soothingly you wound
my soul, in that profundity and center
you once made chaos of!
Only consume it soon,
tearing the veil away in love's encounter.

O cautery that freshens!
O treasure of a wound!
Caresses light as air! considerate palm
with settlement past measure!
(fragrance of heaven around!)
Slaying, you lift us living from the tomb.

O lamps of fire, whose light
streams in the cavernous soul:
through mighty hollows, dazzled from above
(once blind in a blank night)
visiting splendor rolls
lavishing warmth and brilliance on their love.

Oh how serene, how loving
here in my hidden breast
waking in crannies you are master of!
With your affectionate breathing
all health and heavenly rest
how delicately I'm caught afire with love!

COPLAS DEL MISMO
hechas sobre un estasi de harta contempla-
cion

Entreme donde no supe
y quedeme, no sabiendo
toda sciençia traçendiendo.

Yo no supe donde entraua,
pero quando alli me vi,
sin saber donde me estaua
grandes cosas entendi.
no dirè lo que senti
que me quede no sabiendo
toda sciençia traçendiendo.

De paz, y de piedad
era la sciencia perfecta
en profunda soledad
entendida, (via recta)
era cosa tan secreta
que me quede balbuciendo
toda sciencia tracendiendo

Estaua tan embeuido
tan absorto y agenado
que se quedo mi sentido
de todo sentir priuado
y el espiritu dotado
de un entender no entendiendo
toda sciencia tracendiendo.

DEEP RAPTURE
Rimes
after an ecstasy of profound contemplation

I entered who knows where,
knew nothing being there,
burst the mind's barrier.

I entered—where, who knows?—
but being where I would
(where, who dare suppose?)
great things understood
no telling if I could.
Knew nothing being there,
burst the mind's barrier.

Of holiness and peace
profundities I knew;
solitude wide as space
and one road leading true,
farseen but lost too.
Speech failed: being there
burst the mind's barrier.

Head swimming with delight,
all-engrossed and fey—
warders of sound and sight
lay as the dead lay.
My soul in a strange ray
knew all and nothing there—
burst the mind's barrier.

El que alli llega de uero
de si mismo desfallesce
quanto sabia primero
mucho baxo le paresçe
y su sciencia tanto cresce
que se queda no sabiendo
toda sciencia tracendiendo.

Quanto mas alto se sube
tanto menos se entendia
que es la tenebrosa nube
que a la noche esclarecia
por eso quien la sabia
queda siempre no sabiendo
toda sciençia tracendiendo

Este saber no sabiendo
es de tan alto poder
que los sabios arguyendo
jamas le pueden uencer
que lo llega su saber
a no entender entendiendo
toda sciencia tracendiendo.

Y es de tan alta excellencia
aqueste sumo saber
que no ay facultad, ni sciençia
que le puedan emprender

Once there (the dregs of self
bleeding in shock away)
the clever treat as chaff
triumphs of yesterday.
Insight at wider play
knows nothing being there,
bursts the mind's barrier.

With height on height allowed,
less could I say outright
how blackness of one cloud
was a great moon at night.
Who penetrates it quite
knows nothing being there,
bursts the mind's barrier.

This knowing that unknows
has mastery so great,
what pundit would oppose
but boggles in debate?—
being no such advocate
as know not knowing there,
burst the mind's barrier.

A sky-descended kind—
such eminence of thought
no deep-manoeuvering mind
stumbled on or wrought.

quien se supiere uencer
con un no saber sabiendo
yra siempre tracendiendo

Y si lo quereis oyr
consiste esta suma sciencia
en un subido sentir
de la diuinal essencia
es obra de su clemencia
hazer quedar no entendiendo
toda sciençia tracendiendo

souls beyond selfhood caught
know, not knowing, there:
burst the mind's barrier.

If any long for news
of the soul's noblest mode:
What is it? Why infused
vision of very God!—
whose gentleness allowed
wise unknowing there:
burst the mind's barrier.

COPLAS DEL ALMA
que pena por uer a Dios, de el mis
mo aucthor.

Viuo sin viuir en mi
y de tal manera espero
que muero porque no muero

En mi yo no uiuo ya
y sin Dios biuir no puedo
pues sin el, y sin mi quedo
este biuir que serà?
mil muertes se me harà
pues mi misma vida espero
muriendo porque no muero.

Esta vida que yo viuo
es priuacion de biuir
y assi es contino morir
hasta que biua contigo
oye mi Dios lo que digo
que esta uida no la quiero
que muero porque no muero.

Estando absente de ti,
que vida puedo tener?
sino muerte padescer
la mayor que nunca vi.
lastima tengo de mi
pues de suerte persevero
que muero porque no muero

LIFE NO LIFE
Rimes of the soul
in an agony of longing to see God

Living, and no life in me?
languish in expectancy?—
dying to my dying day.

Life within me? No, no spark.
Without God is darkest dark!
Failing him and failing me
how can any life but be
in extremis momently?
Yearning for my life I say:
dying to my dying day!

Seeing that what life I know
has the face of death to show,
and that dying's all I do
till I come alive in you,
hearken to a suitor sue
from a life he'd cast away—
dying to my dying day.

When I'm separate from you,
how to manage? what to do?
Why encourage breath on breath
and sink deeper in my death?
Pity me on this sad path
where, though creeping still, I stay
dying to my dying day.

El pez que del agua sale
aun de aliuio no caresce
que en la muerte que padesce
al fin la muerte le vale
que muerte aura que se yguale
a mi biuir lastimero
pues si mas viuo mas muero.

Quando me pienso a aliuiar
de uerte en el sacramento
hazeme mas sentimiento
el no te poder gozar
todo es para mas penar
por no verte como quiero
y muero porque no muero

Y si me gozo señor
con esperanca de uerte
en ver que puedo perderte
se me dobla mi dolor
viuiendo en tanto pauor
y esperando como espero
muerome porque no muero

Sacame de aquesta muerte
mi Dios y dame la uida
no me tengas impedida
en este lazo tan fuerte

Fish inveigled from the sea
have relief in misery—
in the dying they endure
death's an everpresent cure.
But what end is torture more
than the penalty I pay,
dying to my dying day?

When I hope to find content
and see you in the sacrament,
suddenly I sink heartsore—
not enjoy where I adore?
Here's one injury the more.
Never see you!—that's to say,
dying to my dying day.

Dreaming of elysium, lord,
in hope's vision of reward,
seeing I might never see
doubles my anxiety
till a terror seizes me.
Then I sigh the time away
dying to my dying day.

From this death deliver me;
give life in sweet charity!
No more trussing head and toe
with hard nooses to undo

mira que peno por verte
y mi mal es tan entero
que muero porque no muero

Llorare mi muerte ya
y lamentaré mi vida
en tanto que detenida
por mis peccados està
o mi Dios quando serà
quando yo diga de vero
viuo ya porque no muero

(and my heart afire for you!).
More and more the trammels weigh—
dying to my dying day.

Sorrow for this life I will,
and lament this dying still,
long as I a prisoner in
living make return for sin.
Lord, imploring, when oh when
can I triumph?—Death, away!
life's an everlasting day!

OTRAS DEL MISMO A
lo diuino

Tras de un amoroso lançe
y no de esperança falto
bolé tan alto tan alto
que le di a la caça alcançe

Para que yo alcance diese
a aqueste lance diuino
tanto bolar me conuino
que de vista me perdiese
y con todo en este trançe
en el buelo quedé falto
mas el amor fue tan alto
que le di a la caça alcançe

Quando mas alto subia
deslumbrôseme la vista
y la mas fuerte conquista
en escuro se hacia,
mas por ser de amor el lance
di un ciego y oscuro salto
y fui tan alto tan alto
que le di a la caça alcançe

Quanto mas alto llegaua
de este lançe tan subido
tanto mas bajo, y rendido
y abatido me hallaua
Dixe no aura quien alçançe

OF FALCONRY
a lo divino

A falcon, no feather adroop,
oversailing the heron of love
in thrilling crescendo above:
—a prize!—on the plumage I swoop!

To pounce on the bird quick and true
in flurries of high interplay,
I soared by so dizzy a way
I was barely a guess in the blue.
Even so, at the zenith of hope
I hung numb, until buoyant on love
in thrilling crescendo above
—a prize!—on the plumage I swoop!

At the dizziest pitch of my flight,
my eyes!—they were dazzled and blind.
So my magnificent find
was made amid thickness of night.
Without knowing how, I swung up
(for at stake was a trophy of love)
in thrilling crescendo above
till—a prize!—on the plumage I swoop!

As higher and higher I rose
in sudden and surging ascent,
the more I was conscious *I can't*,
the weaker and weaker I was
and despaired of the quarry: no hope

y abatime tanto tanto
que fui tan alto tan alto
que le di a la caça alcançe

Por una estraña manera
mil buelos passe de un buelo
porque esperança de çielo
tanto alcança quanto espera
esperè solo este lançe
y en esperar no fui falto
pues fui tan alto tan alto
que le di a la caça alcançe

for any pursuer!—and dove
in thrilling crescendo above
till—a prize!—on the plumage I swoop!

Who knows how it ends or begins?
One flight? or a thousand I fly?
Who longs for delight in the sky
whatever he challenges, wins.
Here's no misadventure of hope
(high hope for the heron of love):
in thrilling crescendo above
—a prize!—on the plumage I swoop!

OTRAS CANCIONES
A lo diuino (de el mismo autor)
De Christo y el alma.

Un pastorcico solo esta penado
    ageno de plazer y de contento
    y en su pastora puesto el pensamiento
    y el pecho del amor muy lastimado
    No llora por auerle amor llegado
    que no le pena verse asi afligido
    aunque en el coraçon esta herido
    mas llora por pensar que esta oluidado

Que solo de pensar que esta oluidado
    de su bella pastora con gran pena
    se dexa maltratar en tierra agena
    el pecho de el amor muy lastimado
    Y dize el pastorcico, ay desdichado
    de aquel que de mi amor a hecho ausencia
    y no quiere gozar la mi presencia
    y el pecho por su amor muy lastimado.

Y acabo de un gran rato se a encumbrado
    sobre un arbol: do abrio sus braços bellos
    y muerto se a quedado asido dellos
    el pecho de el amor muy lastimado.

MADRIGAL
A lo divino:
of Christ and the soul

Once a young shepherd went off to despond:
how could he dance again? how could he sing?
All of his thoughts to his shepherdess cling,
with love in his heart like a ruinous wound.

The root of his sorrow? No, never the wound:
the lad was a lover and welcomed the dart
that lodged where it drank the red race of his heart—
but spurned by his fairest, went off to despond.

For only to think he was spurned, and by one
radiant shepherdess, drove him afar;
cost him a drubbing in foreigners' war,
with love in his heart like a ruinous wound.

The shepherd boy murmured: O murrain descend
on the traitor estranging my angel and me!
charming her vision that stares stonily
on the love in my heart like a ruinous wound.

Time passed: on a season he sprang from the ground,
swarmed a tall tree and arms balancing wide
beautifully grappled the tree till he died
of the love in his heart like a ruinous wound.

CANTAR DE LA ALMA
que se huelga de conoscer a Dios
por fee.

Que bien se yo la fonte, que mana, y corre:
    aunque es de noche.

Aquella eterna fonte esta ascondida
    que bien se yo do tiene su manida
    aunque es de noche.

Su origen no lo se, pues no le tiene;
    mas se que todo origen della viene,
    aunque es de noche.

Se que no puede ser cosa tan bella
    y que cielos y tierra beuen della
    aunque es de noche.

Bien se que suelo en ella no se halla
    y que ninguno puede vadealla
    aunque es de noche.

Su claridad nunca es escurecida
    y se que toda luz de ella es uenida
    aunque es de noche.

Se ser tan caudalosos sus corrientes
    que ynfiernos, cielos riegan, y las gentes
    aunque es de noche.

El corriente que nace desta fuente
    bien se que es tan capaz y omnipotente
    aunque es de noche.

SONG OF THE SOUL
whose pleasure is in knowing God
by faith

The spring that brims and ripples oh I know
    in dark of night.

Waters that flow forever and a day
through a lost country—oh I know the way
    in dark of night.

Its origin no knowing, for there's none.
But well I know, from here all sources run
    in dark of night.

Such deep delight what other sight can give?
Here earth and the wide heavens drink to live
    in dark of night.

No fording such a torrent—that I know.
No soundings would discover banks below
    in dark of night.

Waters like crystal luminous forever:
the wellhead of all splendor whatsoever
    in dark of night.

Bounty of waters flooding from this well
invigorate all earth, high heaven, and hell
    in dark of night.

The current this oasis gave birth to
broadens and swells and all it would, can do
    in dark of night.

El corriente que de estas dos procede
    se que ninguna de ellas le precede
    aunque es de noche.

Aquesta eterna fonte esta escondida
    en este viuo pan por darnos vida
    aunque es de noche.

Aqui se esta llamando a las criaturas
    y de esta agua se hartan aunque a escuras
    porque es de noche.

Aquesta biua fuente que desseo
    en este pan de vida yo la ueo
    aunque de noche.

Three merging currents of the living sea
each born of each, none lesser in degree
   in dark of night.

O fountain surging to submerge again
deep in the living bread that's life to men
   in dark of night.

Song of the waters calling: come and drink.
Come, all you creatures, to the shadowy brink
   in dark of night.

This spring of living water I want so,
here in the bread of life I see it flow
   in dark of night.

ROMANCE SOBRE EL
euangelio in principio erat verbum acerca
De la sanctissima trinidad.

En el principio moraua

el uerbo y en Dios biuia

en quien su felicidad

ynfinita posseŷa

el mismo verbo dios era

que el principio se dezia

el moraua en el principio

y principio no tenia

el era el mesmo principio

por eso de el carecia

el verbo se llama hijo

que de el principio nacia

a le siempre concebido

y siempre le concebia

dale siempre su substancia

y siempre se la tenia

y assi la gloria del hijo

es la que en el padre auia

y toda su gloria el padre

en el hijo posseya

como amado en el amante

vno en otro residia

y aquese amor que los une

en lo mismo conuenia

BALLAD I: IN PRINCIPIO
On the most holy trinity

In the beginning the Word
lived in the being of God.
Happy? Oh infinitely!
Therein its happiness had.

Seeing it was God, the Word
(as the beginning we call).
In the beginning it lived;
had no beginning at all.

For the beginning it was;
hence what it was, had not.
Son is the word for the Word
of the beginning begot.

The father, time out of mind
begetting, begets him today:
all he possesses, confers;
giving, gives nothing away.

And where is the soul of the son?
Shown in the father alone.
And the father is where? In the son.
So each has come into his own,

as in the lover the loved—
one in the other is so.
This love interfusing the two
may in equality go

con el uno y con el otro
en ygualdad y ualia
Tres personas y un amado
entre todos tres auia
y un amor en todas ellas
y un amante las hazia
y el amante es el amado
en que cada qual viuia
que el ser que los tres posseen
cada qual le poseia
y cada qual de ellos ama
a la que este ser tenia
este ser es cada una
y este solo las unia
en un inefable nudo
que dezir no se sabia
por lo qual era infinito
el amor que las unia
porque un solo amor tres tienen
que su essencia se dezia
que el amor quanto mas uno
tanto mas amor hazia

both with the one as the one—
level in pitch and degree.
Three are the persons, their love
wonderful one-among-three.

Only one love among three!
One love fathering three!
There where the loved is the lover,
life-giving life to the three!

Reckon the range of their power—
each has it all, and alone.
Each is in love with his loving
peers of the luminous zone.

Each is almighty and all,
each and alone is the tie
of the inscrutable union
staggering *wherefore* and *why*.

Infinite withy and link
is the love celebrated above:
love, sole and yet triple
(such is the mystery thereof);
love, the more single and only,
generates all the more love!

De la comunicacion de las tres personas
2.°

En aquel amor inmenso
que de los dos procedia
palabras de gran regalo
el padre al hijo dezia
de tan profundo deleyte
que nadie las entendia
solo el hijo lo gozaua
que es a quien pertenecia
pero aquello que se entiende
desta manera dezia
nada me contenta hijo
fuera de tu compañia
y si algo me contenta
en ti mismo lo queria
el que a ti mas se parece
a mi mas satisfazia
y el que nada te semeja
en mi nada hallaria
en ti solo me e agradado
o vida de vida mia.
eres lumbre de mi lumbre
eres mi sabiduria
figura de mi substancia
en quien bien me complacia

BALLAD II: OF A COMMUNICATION

In the crescendo of love
that rose from the wonderful two,
the father favored the son
with news of enchanting ado,

inferring a rapture so rich
nobody half understood
but the son, with a jubilant ear
catching what nobody could.

The drift of the father was this
(as near as a mortal can say):
Nothing is sweet to me, son,
when my pride and joy is away.

Whatever's a mine of delight
is lovable only in you.
Any hint of your face in a stranger
is a charm to encircle him too.

Features foreign to yours
in me scant charity find.
My pleasure is all your pleasure,
life of the life that is mine!

Light of the light I live by,
knowledge of all I know,
my intimate nature's double—
and my joy in approving you so!

al que a ti te amare hijo
a mi mismo le daria.
y el amor que yo en ti tengo
esse mismo en el pondria
en razon de auer amado
a quien yo tanto queria.

Whoever is your admirer,
son, he has won my heart;
the love that I lavish on you
he shall have, parcel and part:
seeing he loves whom I love
from the depths of my heart.

De la creacion Romance Tercero
Rom. 3.°

Una esposa que te ame
mi hijo darte queria
que por tu ualor meresca
tener nuestra compania
y comer pan a una mesa
de el mesmo que yo comia
por que conosca los bienes
que en tal hijo yo tenia
y se congracie conmigo
de tu gracia y loçania
muncho lo agradesco padre
el hijo le respondia
a la esposa que me dieres
yo mi claridad daria
para que por ella vea
quanto mi padre ualia
y como el ser que posseo
de su ser le recibia
reclinarla e yo en mi braço
y en tu amor se abrasaria
y con eterno deleyte
tu bondad sublimaria.

BALLAD III: OF THE CREATION

My heart dreams of your having,
son, an affectionate bride,
who for the worthiness in you
merits a place at our side:

to break bread at this table,
the same loaf as we two,
and ripen in acquaintance
with traits I always knew,
with handsome ways and graces—
and prize them as I do.

O father, a world of thanks,
the son to the father replied.
The depth of my luminous gaze
I give as a gift to the bride;

I'd have her use it to see
the kind of father you are:
how all that I have to my name
I have from my luckiest star.

To think she will lie in my arms!
Be warmed in the noons of your love!
and in ecstasy never to end
lift radiant paeans above!

Prosigue 4.°

Hagase pues dixo el padre
que tu amor lo merecia
y en este dicho que dixo
el mundo criado auia
palacio para la esposa
hecho en gran sabiduria
El qual en dos aposentos
alto, y bajo diuidia
el bajo de diferencias
infinitas componia
mas el alto hermoseaua
de admirable pedreria
por que conosca la esposa
el esposo que tenia
en el alto collocaua
la angelica gerarchia
pero la natura humana
en el baxo la ponia
por ser en su compostura
algo de menor valia
y aunque el ser y los lugares
de esta suerte los partia
pero todos son un cuerpo
de la esposa que dezia

BALLAD IV: OF THE CREATION

Amen, the father smiled;
how love's a cajoler in you.
No sooner said than lo!—
the universe sprang to view.

There was a home for the bride!
a pleasure-house cunningly made!
quarters above and below!
two great levels arrayed!

The lower boldly baroque,
a maze of infinite ways.
The upper thrilling and strange,
diamond dust in a blaze.

To show how noble a groom
(should the bride have a shadow of doubt)
in choirs the father banked
flights of angels about.

Apartments close to the ground
he marked for the race of man—
having fewer pretensions to rise,
what in the dust began.

Though the palace and all of its gear
the father chose to divide,
they are one: as single a body
as the body itself of the bride.

que el amor de un mesmo esposo
vna esposa los hazia
los de arriba posseian
el esposo en alegria
Los de abajo en esperança
de fee que les infundia
diziendoles que algun tiempo
el los engrandeceria
y que aquella su baxeza
el se la leuantaria
de manera que ninguno
ya la vituperaria
porque en todo semejante
el a ellos se haria
y se uendria con ellos
y con ellos moraria
y que Dios seria hombre
y que el hombre Dios seria
y trataria con ellos
comeria y beueria
y que con ellos contino
el mismo se quedaria
hasta que se consumase
este siglo que corria

It was one he loved, that lover;
he had eyes for one.
Oh the angels called him truelove
close to their jubilant sun!

Truelove, the earthlings murmured
in hope (with faith for root).
The groom saw, in time future,
radiant changes wrought.

He vowed their meager condition
would be mended: amended so
that none till time had an ending
would find a gibe to throw.

Said he would share their station;
said he would breathe their breath;
mingle in all their dealings;
said he would die the death;

God would be man forever;
man would be God-in-man;
weather our hurlyburly,
fed from trencher and can!

Faithful forever, God said;
vowed to be still the same
till the world that trickles away like sand
flare in a waste of flame.

cuando se gozaran juntos
en eterna melodia
Porque el era la cabeça
de la esposa que tenia
a la qual todos los miembros
de los justos juntaria
que son cuerpo de la esposa
a la qual el tomaria
en sus braços tiernamente
y alli su amor la daria
y que assi juntos en uno
al padre la lleuaria
donde de el mesmo deleyte
que Dios goza, gozaria
que como el padre y el hijo
y el que dellos procedia
el uno viue en el otro
assi la esposa seria
que dentro de Dios absorta
vida de Dios viuiria

Something to sing for, that day!
never a dying fall!
He is the bride's best wisdom—
all of her all-in-all.

Limbs by the world far scattered
whole and together awake;
these are his truelove's body;
these will the lover take

into his two arms, soft oh soft,
confiding an idyll of love,
holding her close, to lift her
high to the father above,

there to be rapt as God is,
seized with the same delight—
for even as father and son
and the third in his outward flight

one in the other endure,
so with the fond and fair—
caught into God's great being,
breathing his very air!

Prosigue 5.° R.^{ce}

Con esta buena esperança
que de ariba les uenia
el tedio de sus trauajos
mas leue se les hazia
pero la esperança larga
y el desseo que crecia
de gozarse con su esposo
contino les afligia
por lo qual con oraciones
con sospiros y agonia
con lagrimas y gemidos
le rogauan noche y dia
que ya se determinase
a les dar su compañia
unos dezian o si fuese
en mi tiempo el alegria
otros acaba señor
al que as de embiar, enbia
otros o si ya rompieses
esos cielos y veria
con mis ojos que bajases
y mi llanto cesaria
regad nubes de lo alto
que la tierra lo pedia

BALLAD V:
OF HUNGER FOR THE COMING

Living in lively hope
with that good news from the sky,
earth saw the peonage days
pass more passably by.

Oh but hope is a humdrum food
and love is a raging fire!
The bride who would glow with the groom
knew anguish of desire.

Praying and praying again,
sighing and wan with pain,
weeping and weeping again,
night and day to exclaim

that he make up his mind and come,
join with her right away.
You could hear: O lucky love,
if I live to see the day!

You could hear: Oh it's long enough!
You know you must come—then come!
You could hear: if a thunderclap
split heaven this minute, and him

I saw with my very eyes!—
no more misery then.
Oh the earth is a dry mouth begging.
Clouds, uncargo the rain!

y abrase ya la tierra
que espinas nos producia
y produzga aquella flor
con que ella floreceria
otros dezian o dichoso
el que en tal tiempo seria
que meresca ver a Dios
con los ojos que tenia
y tratarle con sus manos
y andar en su compañia
y gozar de los mysterios
que entonces ordenaria.

Clay earth, cleave you open,
finish with thistle and thorn.
The flower that makes all earth floral—
time for the flower to be born.

You could hear: O lucky lucky
lovers to see that day—
with your own eyes your lover
hastening your way;

stand near enough to touch him,
brush by his very side,
when that mysterious stranger
hints what the night shall hide.

Prosigue 6.° R.ce

En aquestos y otros ruegos
gran tiempo pasado auia
pero en los prosteros años
el feruor muncho crecia
quando el viejo simeon
en deseo se encendia
Rogando a Dios que quisiese
dexalle uer este dia
y assi el espiritu santo
al buen viejo respondia
que le daua su palabra
que la muerte no ueria
hasta que la vida uiese
que de arriba decendia
y que el en sus mismas manos
al mismo Dios tomaria
y le tendria en sus braços
y consigo abraçaria.

BALLAD VI: OF SIMEON

Well, in appeals like these
a heavy time went by,
but as the hour drew near
fever-heat ran high;

Simeon, good old man,
love-longing all on fire,
implored that he see the day;
called it his one desire.

Therefore the spirit of God
to the good old man averred
he would never see death at all
(the strange voice gave its word)

till he looked on life itself
and saw the gift from the sky;
swore that the good old man
would dandle the marvelous boy;
that the child embraced in his arms,
in his own two arms would lie.

Prosigue la encar.^{on} R.^e 7.º

Ya que el tiempo era llegado
en que hacerse convenia
el rescate de la esposa
que en duro yugo seruia
debajo de aquella ley
que Moyses dado le auia
El padre con amor tierno
desta manera dezia
ya ues hijo que a tu esposa
a tu ymagen hecho auia
y en lo que a ti se pareçe
contigo bien convenia
pero difiere en la carne
que en tu simple ser no auia
en los amores perfectos
esta ley se requeria
que se haga semejante
el amante a quien queria
que la mayor semejança
mas deleyte contenia
el qual sin duda en tu esposa
grandemente creceria
si te viere semejante
en la carne que tenia

BALLAD VII: OF THE INCARNATION

Now as the season approached
(the date love specified)
for the ransom paid in full,
the shackles struck from the bride

who was forfeit under the law
law-giver Moses made,
the father with melting heart
after this fashion said:

My son, I have found you a bride
of your very sort, you'll find.
You will have good cause to know
you are two of a noble kind,

differing only in flesh
(what are you but a child of sky?).
But the course of true love hints
here is a law will apply:

lovers long to become
as identical as they may;
for the more the two are one,
gayer the gala day.

Delight and love in the bride
speedily would increase
(no question at all, my son)
if she saw you a man of flesh.

mi voluntad es la tuya
El hijo le respondia
y la gloria que yo tengo
es tu voluntad ser mia
y a mi me conviene padre
lo que tu alteza dezia
porque por esta manera
tu bondad mas se veria
verase tu gran potencia
justiçia y sabiduria
yrelo a dezir al mundo
y noticia le daria
de tu belleza y dulçura
y de tu soberania
yre a buscar a mi esposa
y sobre mi tomaria
sus fatigas y trauajos
en que tanto padescia
y porque ella vida tenga
yo por ella moriria
y sacandola de el lago
a ti te la bolueria.

I have no will but yours,
the son to the father replied.
The glories of my estate
must on your motion ride.

It couldn't be other than just
I follow as you provide.
How better let all men see
your prevalence far and wide?

How better blazon your might,
sweet reason and deep mind?
I'll carry word to the world,
news of a novel kind:
news of beauty and peace,
range without limit assigned.

I go to be close to the bride
and to take on my back (for it's strong)
the weight of the worldweary toil
that bent the poor back for so long.

To make certain-sure of her life
I'll manfully die in her place,
and drawing her safe from the pit
present her alive to your face.

Prosigue 8.º R^{ce}

Entonces llamó a un archangel
que Sant Gabriel se dezia
y enbiolo a una donzella
que se llamaua maria
de cuyo consentimiento
el mysterio se hazia
en la qual la trinidad
de carne al uerbo vestia
y aunque tres hazen la obra
en el uno se hazia
y quedo el uerbo encarnado
en el vientre de maria
y el que tenia solo padre
ya tambien madre tenia
aunque no como qualquiera
que de varon concebia
que de las entrañas de ella
el su carne recibia
por lo qual hijo de Dios
y de el hombre se dezia

BALLAD VIII: OF THE ANNUNCIATION

It was an angel he beckoned;
it was Gabriel came;
he waved him away on an errand
to Mary—treasure the name.

She must say the right word, this maiden,
for the wonder of wonders to be;
for the Word to be sleeved and gaitered
in flesh by the mighty three.

Three had a hand in the work,
but it worked an effect on one.
Who but the Word made flesh?
Where but in Mary's womb?

The son had a father before;
first had a mother then.
Mother yes, but no mother
conceiving as mothers of men.

He had his flesh of her flesh:
so a new life began.
Now the son of the highest
answers to son of man.

Del nacim.^{to} 9.º R^{ce}.

Ya que era llegado el tiempo
en que de nacer auia
assi como desposado
de su thalamo salia
abraçado con su esposa
que en sus braços la traia
al qual la graciosa madre
en un pesebre ponia
entre unos animales
que a la sazon alli auia
los hombres dezian cantares
los angeles melodia
festejando el desposorio
que entre tales dos auia
Pero Dios en el pesebre
alli lloraua y gemia
que heran joyas : que la esposa
al desposorio traya
y la madre estaua en pazmo
el que tal trueque veia
el llanto de el hombre en dios
y en el hombre la alegria
lo qual de el uno y de el otro
tan ageno ser solia.

finis.

BALLAD IX: OF THE NATIVITY

In time it came round, the time
ripe for the birth of a boy.
Much as a bridegroom steps
fresh from the chamber of joy,

arm in arm he arrived
entwining the sweetheart he chose.
Both in a byre at hand
the pleasant mother reposed

among oxen and burros and such
as the winter sky drove in.
How they struck up a tune, those folk!
Sweeter the angels sang!

There was a bridal to chant!
There was a pair well wed!
But why did he sob and sob,
God in his rough-hewn bed?

Such a dazzle of tears!—this gift
all that the bride could bring?
How the mother was struck at so
topsy-turvy a thing:

distress of the flesh, in God!
in man, the pitch of delight!
Pairs never coupled so;
different as day and night.

finis.

Otro de el mismo que va por su
per flumina Babilonis.

Encima de las corrientes

que en babilonia hallaua

alli me sente llorando

alli la tierra regaua

acordandome de ti

o sion a quien amaua

era dulce tu memoria

y con ella mas lloraua

dexe los trages de fiesta

los de trauajo tomaua

y colgue en los verdes sauzes

la musica que lleuaua

poniendola en esperança

de aquello que en ti esperaua

alli me hirio el amor

y el coraçon me sacaua.

Dixele que me matase

pues de tal suerte llagaua

yo me metia en su fuego

sabiendo que me abrasaua

desculpando al auesica

que en el fuego se acabaua

estauame en mi muriendo

y en ti solo respiraua

BALLAD OF BABYLON
Super flumina Babylonis

Brimming of rivers
by Babylon town—
there I sat weeping,
watered the ground.

You in my thoughts, O
Sion my love.
Pleasure of memory
let the tears prove.

Satin I step from,
don dungaree;
stow the harp high in a
green willow tree.

Stow it in hope there,
looking to you,
archer of hearts—their
ravager too.

Finish your victory!
finish! I cry.
Fell in white embers,
pining to die.

Kept a fond eye on
moths in the flame.
Dying my life, I
lived in your name.

en mi por ti me moria
y por ti resusitaua
que la memoria de ti
daua vida i la quitaua
gozauanse los estraños
entre quien catiuo estaua
preguntauanme cantares
de lo que en sion cantaua
canta de Sion un hymno
veamos como sonaua
dezid como en tierra agena
donde por Sion lloraua
cantare yo el alegria
que en Sion se me quedaua
echariala en oluido
si en la agena me gozaua
con mi paladar se junte
la lengua con que hablaua
si de ti yo me oluidare
en la tierra do moraua
Sion por los uerdes ramos
que Babilonia me daua
De mi se oluide mi diestra
que es lo que en ti mas amaua

Dying, died wholly.
Died and awoke.
Lover, your image
tendered and took.

Meanwhile the jocular
jailkeepers crow:
Sing us a Siony
ballad of woe!
Chanties of Sionville—
how do they go?

Mourning my country
in faraway air,
sing to a stranger
Sion so dear?
Harden my heart to her,
high-living here?

Cleave and be clotted,
tongue, to your roof,
when I gaze scornfully,
swagger aloof;

hands, here in Babylon,
wish me a blight,
gesture against me,
even this right,

si de ti no me acordare

en lo que mas me gozaua

y si yo tuuiere fiesta

y sin ti la festejaua

o hija de Babilonia

misera y desuenturada

bien auenturado era

aquel en quien confiaua

que te a de dar el castigo

que de tu mano lleuaua

y juntara sus pequeños

y a mi porque en ti lloraua

a la piedra que era Christo

por el qual yo te dexaua.

Debetur soli gloria vera
Deo.

when I forget you,
Sion my star,
when I go gay here,
fettered so far.

Daughter of Babylon,
dismal and doomed,
here's to a comforter
comes to the land:
girded to wrestle the
rod from your hand,

to settle his nurslings
(soothing my rue)
in the rock's lee—rough
durance, adieu!

To God alone, true
glory.

II

ADDITIONAL POEMS

GLOSA A LO DIVINO

Sin arrimo y con arrimo,
Sin luz y a oscuras viviendo,
Todo me voy consumiendo.

Mi alma está desasida
De toda cosa criada,
Y sobre sí levantada,
Y en una sabrosa vida,
Sólo en su Dios arrimada.
Por eso ya se dirá
La cosa que más estimo,
Que mi alma se ve ya
Sin arrimo y con arrimo.

Y aunque tinieblas padezco
En esta vida mortal,
No es tan crecido mi mal;
Porque, si de luz carezco,
Tengo vida celestial;
Porque el amor de tal vida,
Cuando más ciego va siendo,
Que tiene al alma rendida,
Sin luz y a oscuras viviendo.

Hace tal obra el amor,
Después que le conocí,
Que, si hay bien o mal en mí,

WITHOUT AND WITH MAINSTAY
a lo divino

Without and with mainstay,
no lantern, light of day,
burning, I burn away.

My spirit in free flight
breaks from the pull of earth,
tie of its human birth,
to breathe a keen delight
suspended on God's worth.
Let the world hear: I hold
my heart's one wish today,
knowing my very soul
without and with mainstay.

Though shadows haunt me still
from man's shape in the sun,
less plaintively they call—
when joys of daylight pall
my heaven is well begun.
Love of that life is such
it thrives in any way:
blind, humble, led by a touch,
no lantern, light of day.

With governance of charm
love touched my best and worst
till all, even cankered harm,

Todo lo hace de un sabor,
Y al alma transforma en sí;
Y así, en su llama sabrosa,
La cual en mí estoy sintiendo,
Apriesa, sin quedar cosa,
Todo me voy consumiendo.

turn fiber sweet and warm
(being in love immersed).
No wonder resinous fire
leaps sinewy and gay,
as clean to a clean pyre
burning, I burn away.

GLOSA A LO DIVINO DEL MISMO AUTOR

Por toda la hermosura
Nunca yo me perderé,
Si no por un no sé qué
Que se alcanza por ventura.

Sabor de bien que es finito,
Lo más que puede llegar,
Es cansar el apetito
Y estragar el paladar;
Y así, por toda dulzura
Nunca yo me perderé,
Sino por un no sé qué
Que se halla por ventura.

El corazón generoso
Nunca cura de parar
Donde se puede pasar,
Sino en más dificultoso;
Nada le causa hartura,
Y sube tanto su fe,
Que gusta de un no sé qué
Que se halla por ventura.

El que de amor adolece,
Del divino ser tocado,
Tiene el gusto tan trocado,
Que a los gustos desfallece;
Como el que con calentura

THE HUNTER'S QUEST
a lo divino

I'll never pitch away my soul
to clutch at loveliness.
But for a quarry who can tell—
   my life on the hunter's quest!

Crust and crumbs of being,
tang that the tongue can know
are brittles soon decaying:
bait for the body's woe.
I'll never pitch away my soul
to cuddle lusciousness,
but for a quarry who can tell—
   my life on the hunter's quest!

What great-of-heart's for lagging
where packs of stragglers go?
What buoyant soul for dragging
bottomlands below?
Gay hunters on the hill
never rein for rest,
but scenting a quarry who can tell—
   my life on the hunter's quest!

As lovers bright with longing
(for love of Love aglow)
despond if fun come fawning,
their joy's converted so;
as planks of food repel

Fastidia el manjar que ve,
Y apetece un no sé qué
Que se halla por ventura.

No os maravilléis de aquesto,
Que el gusto se quede tal,
Porque es la causa del mal
Ajena de todo el resto;
Y así, toda criatura
Enajenada se ve,
Y gusta de un no sé qué
Que se halla por ventura.

Que estando la voluntad
De Divinidad tocada,
No puede quedar pagada
Sino con Divinidad;
Mas, por ser tal su hermosura,
Que sólo se ve por fe,
Gústala en un no sé qué
Que se halla por ventura.

Pues de tal enamorado,
Decidme si habréis dolor,
Pues que no tiene sabor
Entre todo lo criado;
Sólo, sin forma y figura,
Sin hallar arrimo y pie,

men by malaria tossed—
sick for a quarry who can tell
    my life on the hunter's quest!

No need to be exclaiming
if these are minded so—
their balsam, the best flaming,
is nowhere here below.
Nor fellow warmth, though all
rove for it east and west.
But for a quarry who can tell—
    my life on the hunter's quest!

The will of a man thrilling
to a far trumpet tone—
all's over: no fulfilling
but in love alone.
Toward whose citadel
faith and her rangers press,
off for a quarry who can tell—
    my life on the hunter's quest!

That suitor of your choosing,
say: do humors grow
downcast at refusing
gusto of things below?
No purchase (step or sill)
but hobbling, lopped of flesh,

Gustando allá un no sé qué
Que se halla por ventura.

No penséis que el interior,
Que es de mucha más valía,
Halla gozo y alegría
En lo que acá da sabor;
Mas sobre toda hermosura,
Y lo que es y será y fué,
Gusta de allá un no sé qué
Que se halla por ventura.

Más emplea su cuidado
Quien se quiere aventajar,
En lo que está por ganar,
Que en lo que tiene ganado;
Y así, para más altura
Yo siempre me inclinaré
Sobre todo a un no sé qué
Que se halla por ventura.

Por lo que por el sentido
Puede acá comprehenderse,
Y todo lo que entenderse,
Aunque sea muy subido,
Ni por gracia y hermosura
Yo nunca me perderé,
Sino por un no sé qué
Que se halla por ventura.

after a quarry who can tell—
   my life on the hunter's quest!

Do any think this yearning
banked in the golden soul
would leap elate, returning
to the bare native shoal?
No season did or will
wheedle the heart to rest,
but for a quarry who can tell—
   my life on the hunter's quest!

Whose dogged yen's for perching
on material store,
nods to tomorrow urging:
more! get more and more!
So I—an airier tale—
adventure crest to crest
intent on a quarry who can tell—
   my life on the hunter's quest!

Not for all knowledge, throwing
wider the fivefold door,
or gales of the spirit blowing
high as a thought can soar,
I'll never pitch away my soul,
and not for loveliness:
but for a quarry who can tell—
   my life on the hunter's quest!

DEL VERBO DIVINO

Del Verbo divino
La Virgen preñada
Viene de camino
Si le dais posada.

SUMA DE LA PERFECCIÓN

Olvido de lo criado,
Memoria del Criador,
Atención a lo interior
Y estarse amando al Amado.

DIVINE WORD

The wayfaring virgin,
Word in her womb,
comes walking your way—
haven't you room?

THE CAPSULE OF PERFECTION

The whole of creation forgotten;
its Maker remembered forever.
Inward the gaze of the spirit,
forever in love with the Lover.

III

FROM THE CODEX
OF JAÉN

CANCIONES ENTRE EL ALMA Y EL ESPOSO

ESPOSA

¿A dónde te escondiste,
Amado, y me dejaste con gemido?
Como el ciervo huiste,
Habiéndome herido;
Salí tras ti clamando, y eras ido.

Pastores, los que fuerdes
Allá por las majadas al otero,
Si por ventura vierdes
Aquel que yo más quiero,
Decilde que adolezco, peno y muero.

Buscando mis amores,
Iré por esos montes y riberas,
Ni cogeré las flores,
Ni temeré las fieras,
Y pasaré los fuertes y fronteras.

PREGUNTA A LAS CRIATURAS

¡Oh, bosques y espesuras,
Plantadas por la mano del Amado!
¡Oh, prado de verduras,
De flores esmaltado,
Decid si por vosotros ha pasado!

THE SPIRITUAL CANTICLE
Songs between the soul and the bridegroom

THE BRIDE

Where have you hidden away?
Never a crumb of comfort day or night,
dearest? To wound your prey
and off like a stag in flight!
I hurried forth imploring you—out of sight!

You shepherds, you that rove
up in the ranches on the mountain's brow,
if you should meet my love,
my one love, tell him how
I'm heartsick, fevered, and fast sinking now.

I'll go myself and scour
highland and lowland over for my dear;
not dawdle for a flower;
no fang of prowler fear;
bursting by each confronter and frontier.

A QUESTION TO THE CREATURES

O groves and leafy screen,
foliage planted by a lover's hand,
meadows of bluegreen
with marigolds japanned,
tell me, has he been lately in your land?

RESPUESTA DE LAS CRIATURAS

Mil gracias derramando,
Pasó por estos sotos con presura,
Y yéndolos mirando,
Con sola su figura
Vestidos los dejó de hermosura.

ESPOSA

¡Ay, quién podrá sanarme!
Acaba de entregarte ya de vero,
No quieras enviarme
De hoy más ya mensajero,
Que no saben decirme lo que quiero.

Y todos cuantos vagan,
De ti me van mil gracias refiriendo,
Y todos más me llagan,
Y déjame muriendo
Un no sé qué que quedan balbuciendo.

Mas, ¿cómo perseveras,
Oh vida, no viviendo donde vives,
Y haciendo porque mueras,
Las flechas que recibes,
De lo que del Amado en ti concibes?

¿Por qué, pues has llagado
Aqueste corazón, no le sanaste?
Y pues me le has robado,
¿Por qué así le dejaste,
Y no tomas el robo que robaste?

THEIR RESPONSE

Lavishing left and right
a world of wonders, he went streaming by
these orchards, meteor-bright:
beneath his brilliant eye
rose many a green pavilion to the sky.

THE BRIDE

What cure for my disease?
Give up, give up in earnest. Make an ending.
These tedious deputies,
I beg of you, stop sending:
what good are these—pretending and pretending?

Figures that come and go
bring news of you indeed: what jubilant rumor!
I reel as with a blow;
sink stricken at the glimmer
of something heard ecstatic in the stammer.

Strange! to feel the breath
of life endure, not living where life is.
Brought low and close to death
by those bowmen of his—
to each inroad of love sharp witnesses.

Unready yet to mend
the havoc in this heart—so quick to break it?
Possess and not intend
ever to take it?
Have it by force and forceably forsake it?

Apaga mis enojos,
Pues que ninguno basta a deshacellos,
Y véante mis ojos,
Pues eres lumbre de ellos,
Y sólo para ti quiero tenellos.

Descubre tu presencia,
Y máteme tu vista y hermosura;
Mira que la dolencia
De amor, que no se cura
Sino con la presencia y la figura.

¡Oh, cristalina fuente,
Si en esos tus semblantes plateados,
Formases de repente
Los ojos deseados,
Que tengo en mis entrañas dibujados!

Apártalos, Amado,
Que voy de vuelo.

ESPOSO

Vuélvete, paloma,
Que el ciervo vulnerado
Por el otero asoma,
Al aire de tu vuelo, y fresco toma.

ESPOSA

Mi Amado, las montañas,
Los valles solitarios nemorosos,
Las ínsulas extrañas,
Los ríos sonorosos,
El silbo de los aires amorosos,

Oh shorten the long days
of burning thirst—no other love allays them.
Let my eyes see your face,
treasure to daze them.
Except for love, it's labor lost to raise them.

Appear here at my side.
End me in splendor with a blaze of grace.
Look at love's invalid
heartsick, a failing case—
only one chance of comfort: face to face.

If only, crystal well,
clear in the mirror's silver could arise
suddenly by some spell
the long awaited eyes
the poor heart scrapes in clay to improvise!

Love, cover those bright eyes!
I'm voyaging on air!

THE BRIDEGROOM
Float downward, dove.
The stag from covert lies
hurt on the hill above,
stirred by your wing he loves the coolness of.

THE BRIDE
My love: the mountain's height;
forest ravines and faraway recesses;
torrents' sonorous weight;
isles no explorer guesses;
the affectionate air all whisper and caresses;

La noche sosegada
En par de los levantes del aurora,
La música callada,
La soledad sonora,
La cena_que recrea y enamora.

Cazadnos las raposas,
Que está ya florecida nuestra viña,
En tanto que de rosas
Hacemos una piña,
Y no parezca nadie en la montiña.

Detente, Cierzo muerto;
Ven, Austro, que recuerdas los amores,
Aspira por mi huerto,
Y corran tus olores,
Y pacerá el Amado entre las flores.

¡Oh, ninfas de Judea,
En tanto que en las flores y rosales
El ámbar perfumea,
Morá en los arrabales,
Y no queráis tocar nuestros umbrales!

Escóndete, Carillo,
Y mira con tu haz a las montañas,
Y no quieras decillo;
Mas mira las compañas
De la que va por ínsulas extrañas.

the serene flow of night
with dawn a rising twilight in the skies;
music of still delight;
a desert of sweet cries;
a supper of light hearts and lovelit eyes.

Now that the bloom uncloses
catch us the little foxes by the vine,
as we knit cones of roses
cunning as those of pine.
Let no intruder loom on our skyline.

Dwindle, O wind of death.
Come, southern wind, for lovers; come and stir
the garden with your breath.
Make affluent the air.
My love is gladdened among lilies there.

Girls of Jerusalem,
now that the breath of roses more and more
eddies on leaf and stem,
be stranger than before.
Stand further. And no darkening our door.

And darling, settle here.
Look to the mountain ranges; turn your face.
Hush! nothing in my ear.
But look what crewmen grace
the passer of fabulous islands in her chase.

ESPOSO
A las aves ligeras,
Leones, ciervos, gamos saltadores,
Montes, valles, riberas,
Aguas, aires, ardores
Y miedos de las noches veladores:

Por las amenas liras,
Y canto de serenas os conjuro,
Que cesen vuestras iras,
Y no toquéis al muro,
Porque la Esposa duerma más seguro.

Entrádose ha la Esposa
En el ameno huerto deseado,
Y a su sabor reposa,
El cuello reclinado
Sobre los dulces brazos del Amado.

Debajo del manzano,
Allí conmigo fuiste desposada,
Allí te dí la mano,
Y fuiste reparada
Donde tu madre fuera violada.

ESPOSA
Nuestro lecho florido
De cuevas de leones enlazado,
En púrpura tendido,
De paz edificado,
De mil escudos de oro coronado.

THE BRIDEGROOM
Wings twinkling here and there,
lion and gamboling antler, shy gazelle,
peak, precipice, and shore,
flame, air, and flooding well,
night-watchman terror, with no good to tell—

by many a pleasant lyre
and song of sirens I command you all:
bury this wrangling air;
no nuzzling at the wall.
But let the bride in a deep slumber fall.

She enters, the bride! closes,
soft, the enchanting garden dreams foretold her.
Gracefully she reposes;
my arms enfold her,
her throat affectionate upon my shoulder.

Under the apple tree
the words of our betrothal and their spell:
I took you tenderly,
hurt virgin, made you well
where all the scandal on your mother fell.

THE BRIDE
Our bed: in roses laid,
patrols of lions ranging all around;
of royal purple made,
pitched on halcyon ground,
with blazonry of golden bucklers crowned.

A zaga de tu huella
Las jóvenes discurren al camino
Al toque de centella,
Al adobado vino,
Emisiones de bálsamo divino.

En la interior bodega
De mi amado bebí, y cuando salía
Por toda aquesta vega,
Ya cosa no sabía
Y el ganado perdí que antes seguía.

Allí me dió su pecho,
Allí me enseñó ciencia muy sabrosa,
Y yo le dí de hecho
A mí, sin dejar cosa,
Allí le prometí de ser su esposa.

Mi alma se ha empleado,
Y todo mi caudal en su servicio;
Ya no guardo ganado,
Ni ya tengo otro oficio,
Que ya sólo en amar es mi ejercicio.

Pues ya si en el ejido
De hoy más no fuere vista ni hallada,
Diréis que me he perdido;
Que andando enamorada,
Me hice perdidiza, y fuí ganada.

Breathless, on roads you mark
girls whirl to the four winds; their foreheads shine
stung by a sudden spark,
flushed with delightful wine.
What swirls of fragrance widening and divine!

Shown deeper than before
in cellars of my love I drank; from there
went wandering on the moor;
knew nothing, felt no care;
the sheep I tended once are who knows where?

There he broke secrecy;
had honey of revelation to confide.
There I gave all of me;
put chariness aside:
there I promised to become his bride.

Forever at his door
I gave my heart and soul. My fortune too.
I've no flock any more,
no other work in view.
My occupation: love. It's all I do.

If I'm not seen again
in the old places, on the village ground,
say of me: lost to men.
Say I'm adventure-bound
for love's sake. Lost (on purpose) to be found.

De flores y esmeraldas,
En las frescas mañanas escogidas,
Haremos las guirnaldas,
En tu amor florecidas,
Y en un cabello mío entretejidas.

En solo aquel cabello
Que en mi cuello volar consideraste,
Mirástele en mi cuello,
Y en él preso quedaste,
Y en uno de mis ojos te llagaste.

Cuando tú me mirabas,
Su gracia en mí tus ojos imprimían:
Por eso me adamabas,
Y en eso merecían
Los míos adorar lo que en ti vían!

No quieras despreciarme,
Que si color moreno en mí hallaste,
Ya bien puedes mirarme,
Después que me miraste,
Que gracia y hermosura en mí dejaste.

ESPOSO

La blanca palomica
Al arca con el ramo se ha tornado,
Y ya la tortolica
Al socio deseado
En las riberas verdes ha hallado.

In the cool morning hours
we'll gather many a tender wreath to wear,
with emeralds and dayflowers
sprung in love's summer air.
I'll give for their entwining a lock of hair

    curling upon my shoulder—
you loved to see it lifted on the air.
You loved it, fond beholder
caught fascinated there—
my glance embedded then the barb you wear.

    Your eyes caressing me
fell on their living image in my own
and loved distractedly.
That stirring look alone
gave mettle to return the fervor shown.

    Please, no pitying brow
seeing my cheek was dusky in those days.
Only turn this way now
as once before—that gaze
adorned me fresh and lovely in its rays.

THE BRIDEGROOM
    The little pearl-white dove
with frond of olive to the ark returns.
Wedded, the bird of love
no longer yearns,
nestled above still water, among ferns.

En soledad vivía,
Y en soledad ha puesto ya su nido,
Y en soledad la guía
A solas su querido,
También en soledad de amor herido.

ESPOSA

Gocémonos, Amado,
Y vámonos a ver en tu hermosura
Al monte y al collado,
Do mana el agua pura;
Entremos más adentro en la espesura.

Y luego a las subidas
Cavernas de la piedra nos iremos,
Que están bien escondidas,
Y allí nos entraremos,
Y el mosto de granadas gustaremos.

Allí me mostrarías
Aquello que mi alma pretendía,
Y luego me darías
Allí tú, vida mía,
Aquello que me diste el otro día.

El aspirar del aire,
El canto de la dulce Filomena,
El soto y su donaire,
En la noche serena
Con llama que consume y no da pena.

She spent most lonely days,
in loneliest of regions kept her nest,
her guide on lonesome ways
her love, who knew them best—
that arrow from the desert in his breast.

THE BRIDE

A celebration, love!
Let's revel at both our beauty in your eyes!
To the hill and heights above!
cascades that freshen these!
then further, deep and deeper in the trees.

And on to the steeple rock
all honeycombed with caverns and with mines
well off the common track.
Safe in those high confines
we'll taste the tingle of pomegranate wines.

There finally you'll show
something my soul long wept and waited for,
and the same moment, O
my dearest life, restore
what once upon a time you gave before:

the breathing of the air,
the nightingale in her affectionate vein,
woods and the freshness there
in night's unruffled reign—
these, and the flames embracing without pain.

Que nadie lo miraba,
Aminadab tampoco parecía,
Y el cerco sosegaba,
Y la caballería

None loitering to see:
Aminadab the demon fled affrighted.
The siege sank quietly.
The horsemen sighted
vistas of shining water and alighted.

IV

NOTES

CONSIDERATIONS

I

If we place the name of St. John of the Cross with his poetic peers—in such a list, say, as Sappho, Catullus, Leopardi, Blake, Yeats, Lorca—it would probably look to many of us like the name that least belonged, the name to be struck out in an exercise in categories. It even seems, somehow, the wrong name for a poet. If so, it is not his name; San Juan de la Cruz, his proper oriflamme, is not so pallid. Some of us may think of him with the shiver of distaste William James, badly informed on the subject, evidently felt, or with T. S. Eliot's deep bow of respect for his "devotional monument." St. John of the Cross was a "mystic"—that to many today suggests something suspicious or lurid (as indeed it did to many of his contemporaries). We may connect it with parapsychology or ESP or candles in a darkened room or levitation or hallucinative mushrooms or delusions of the endocrines. On the other hand, we may find the mysticism so dazzling that with Menéndez Pelayo we think it profanation to appraise the poems by literary standards at all—we might even think irrelevant José Pemán's praise of this poetry as "the loftiest peak achieved in any of the romance languages."

If we come with hesitations to the poetry, suppose we let García Lorca introduce us. In his essay on *duende*,* Lorca tells us that there are artists sponsored by an Angel that guides, endows, dazzles, shedding his grace in mid-air. There are those sponsored by the Muse, who comes "bearing landscapes of columns and the false taste of laurel." There is also a third type, which has *duende*: the Andalusian term for

*The quotations from Lorca's essays are from *The Poet in New York*, with translations by Ben Belitt. Grove Press, 1955.

119

that mysterious power "that all may feel and no philosophy may explain," that all Dionysian artists at their best have, the bullfighter "who hurls his heart against the horns" or the flamenco singer "like a woman possessed, her face blasted like a medieval weeper . . . feeling the power rise from the very soles of her feet." *Duende* is

> the mystery, the roots that probe through the mire we all know of, and do not understand, but which furnishes us with whatever is sustaining in art. . . . In all Arabic music, in the dances, songs, elegies of Arabia, the coming of the *Duende* is greeted by fervent outcries of *Allah! Allah! . . .* so close to the *Olé! Olé!* of our bull rings that who is to say they are not actually the same; and in all the songs of southern Spain the appearance of the *Duende* is followed by heartfelt exclamations of *God alive!*— profound, human, tender, the cry of communion with God through the medium of the five senses . . .

St. John of the Cross belongs not with the Angel, as we might suspect, nor with the Muse: taking him with two of the greatest names in Spanish poetry Lorca acclaims him thus: "The Muse of Góngora and the Angel of Garcilaso must yield up the laurel wreath when the *Duende* of St. John of the Cross passes by . . ."

And is it just accidental, the remarkable similarity between the tone and imagery of St. John's greatest poems and Lorca's brilliant account of the poet at work?—

> The poet who embarks on the creation of the poem (as I know by experience), begins with the aimless sensation of a hunter about to embark on a night hunt through the remotest of forests. Unaccountable dread stirs in his heart. . . . Then the poet is off on the chase. Delicate breezes chill the lenses of his eyes. The moon, curved like a horn of soft metal, calls in the silence of the topmost branches. White stags appear in the clearing between the tree trunks. Absolute night withdraws in a curtain of whispers. Water flickers in the reeds, quiet and deep . . . "
> (*The Poetic Image in Don Luis de Góngora*).

Is the effect of this poetry, in which "the sense of flight and thrill and ecstasy," says Gerald Brenan, "has never been equalled by anyone else," explicable in literary terms? Obviously much of it is. There is the vivid vocabulary, astonishingly modern, strong in nouns and verbs, colloquial, dialectal at times, at times even rural, enriched with hieratic echoes of the *Song of Songs*, of the pastorals of Garcilaso, of the romantic diction of the troubadours. In directness and simplicity it reminds us of Sappho, who, perhaps alone of the Greeks, used the very speech she heard around her. The poem to Aphrodite (but not that called "To Anactoria") is, after its opening litany, remarkably like St. John's poetry in richness of sound, directness of address, and especially in the passionate appeal of the long fleet sentences overriding the stanza-breaks—in every respect indeed except imagery, in which the *Duende* of Old Castile quite overbears the *Duende* of the islands.

"Metaphor," wrote Lorca in his essay on Góngora, "links two antagonistic worlds by an equestrian leap of imagination." St. John of the Cross had to link the very extremes of being by expressing the highest in terms of the lowest, the *todo* in terms of the *nada*. Images to express the ineffable must be taken from the physical world and accommodated to the five slant gratings by way of which comes all we know. The very souls through which God passes cannot describe their experience, says St. John in the Prologue to the "Spiritual Canticle," unless "by means of figures, comparisons, and similitudes, they give some inkling of what they feel and of the soul's secret and mysterious resources, rather than a logical explanation." So Dante in the *Paradiso* (following common sense and Aquinas' "traduntur nobis spiritualia sub metaphoris corporalium"):

> Così parlar conviensi al vostro ingegno
> però che solo da sensato apprende
> ciò che fa poscia d'intelletto degno.
> Per questo la Scrittura condescende
> a vostra facultate, e piedi e mano
> attribuisce a Dio, ed altro intende . . .

The voice of Jehovah Himself, speaking to Job out of the whirlwind, could do no better than fall back on the wonders of zoology and meteorology. From the natural order too comes the brilliant phantasmagoria of the *Cántico*, the *Noche*, the *Llama*: a spiritual Alice-in-wonderland of images that arise, enchant, change magically, vanish. All are deeply symbolic, but never lashed into place by the heavy hand of allegory, with its passion for pigeonholing.

A la tarde te examinarán en el amor, wrote St. John in one of his Prayers of the Enamored Soul; by the quality of our love alone is measured the success or failure of our lives. Absorbed chiefly in the love between man and the supreme object of his desire, he may have wondered: what image for this ultimate delight? The poet's equestrian leap took him to the image of human love, as in the *Song of Songs*, certainly his favorite poetry and his favorite part of the Bible. The narrative and imagery of the *Cántico* are based on the pursuit of courtship, the promise of betrothal, the fruition of marriage. Even in his own time the theme must have drawn raised eyebrows from the prim, embarrassed giggles from the forever callow. St. Teresa tells of a sermon on the same theme broken by ignorant chortles from the congregation. She tells too of nuns who were scandalized by the *Song of Songs*:

> You may think that in these Canticles there are some things which could have been said otherwise. Our dullness being what it is, I should not be surprised if you did: I have heard some people say that they actually tried not to listen to them. O God, how miserable is our condition! We are like poisonous things that make poison of all they eat . . . !

But the puritan penumbra had not fallen on St. John of the Cross—it seems never to have occurred to him that the language of human passion might be an improper metaphor for divine love. Nor is he fevered by it; critics have never ceased to wonder at the freshness, sweetness, and delicacy with which he has handled the theme.

Concerned with love as he was, St. John of the Cross realized, more completely and continuously than Dante himself, the famous definition of the *stil nuovo*:

> I' mi son un, che quando
> Amor mi spira, noto, e a quel modo
> ch' e' ditta dentro vo significando.

"*Estas canciones . . .*" he says in the Prologue to the "Spiritual Canticle," "*parecen ser escritas con algún fervor de amor . . .*" And a witness reported how he wrote the last stanzas of the poem "*llevado de este amor.*"

Alike in inspiration, Dante and St. John of the Cross are very different in performance. Dante, even in heaven, is never far from earth: St. John, even on earth, is never far from heaven. Dante may be straining upward with his eyes wide on the sun itself, but look closely: springy beneath his toes is the honest Tuscan sod. There is something fresh and sweet, in the best sense naive, about St. John. Dante is never naive: no one was more worldly-wise than this soldier, scholar, scientist, cosmopolite, diplomat—he lived inextricably in a world that St. John hardly touches on. Italy at the turn of the thirteenth century is everywhere in Dante; as far as sixteenth-century Spain is concerned, St. John might as well have been writing at the very core of Dante's pearl-white moon. Hence the emotional tone is so different in the two. Dante gives us few passages of pure joy—that is not his note. Lines, even love-inspired, are likely to be choked or vibrant, ringing with ambivalent passions. Joy is always close to rage—rage perhaps noble, perhaps partisan. Passages that at first seem idyllic are likely to be touched with melancholy:

> Era già l'ora che volge il disio
> ai navicanti, e 'ntenerisce il core . . .

Perhaps we look forward to perfect joy with the appearance of Beatrice in the *Purgatorio*, but we soon find that, like so many Mediterranean beauties, she can put an edge on her voice faintly embarrassing to the lovely creatures around her. Even in heaven the sainted figures can turn fairly apoplectic with anger and burst into billingsgate. It is tempting to make a case for the poetic superiority of St. John's vision of beatitude—less a work of art than Dante's, but surely more a dazzle of *duende*.

Joy in St. John is excruciatingly keen:

> joy was his song and joy so pure
> a heart of star by him could steer.

He addresses God as a person, loved and loving. This, Dante never brings himself to do; for him, God (most beautifully and tremendously) is *Amore*, but he is not "dear" or "beloved"—much less anything like "*Carillo*" or "Darling."

These differences affect and are affected by language, sound, and rhythm. (That St. John could be a conscious technician is shown by a well-known anecdote: when asked if God directly inspired his words, he answered, as any poet would, "Some times God gave them to me, and other times I had to find them for myself.") His language is less sculptural than Dante's, less a language of reason, of meditation. It is more primary, more primitive, with more than a touch of the orient—with even a hint of Oceanica in the rich vocalizations, the soft, half-obliterated Spanish *d*'s of

> *Amada en el Amado transformada.*

The emotional difference shows itself in the coloring of the verses. Typical of Dante are the great dark vowels with which Farinata breaks his stony silence:

> *O Tosco, che per la città del foco . . .*

and that sometimes give an oddly sombre coloring even to loveliness, as in the lines that describe the sapphire dawn along the shores of Purgatory:

> *Dolce color d'oriental zaffiro . . .*

The vowels, dark-gold or midnight-blue, deeply internal, introspective, belong with something longed for rather than possessed.

In St. John's characteristic tone are the softer, brighter, fleeter sounds of

> *entre las azucenas olvidado . . .*
> *en el ameno huerto deseado . . .*
> *en las riberas verdes ha hallado . . .*

When Dante works in a manner like this, as in

> *Quale ne' plenilunii sereni*
> *Trivïa ride tra le ninfe etterne . . .*

he is slower, more weighty—more artistic, less impulsive. The beauty is just a bit less spontaneous, a bit more constructed. And how different the rhythm!

Dante's rhythm is by no means slow—but he does not have (why should he?) the headlong velocity of St. John. In part the variation of line-length in the *lira* (cf. Notes on "The Spiritual Canticle") makes the difference, but more significant is the structure of the line itself. Dante's hendecasyllable is built around two or three fixed accents—from his basic patterns he departs only for certain extraordinary effects that are one of the marvels of his versification. We might expect the hendecasyllables of St. John, like those of Garcilaso and Fray Luis de León, to be built around accents on the fourth and eighth syllables. But as Dámaso Alonso emphasizes, St. John makes an astonishing departure by balancing his lines invariably on the acme of the sixth syllable (an effect that I doubt can be reproduced in English). His lines, therefore, have an amazing velocity, the perfect medium for the ardor and vehemence of his chase. The difference in speed between the two poets is felt when Dante is otherwise most like St. John, as in his description of the *Paradiso terrestre*: here is an enchanted landscape that might conceivably be St. John's. But in Dante the pace is pensive; we would find a closer parallel, in élan and even in tone, between St. John's manner and the breathless hexameters that describe the garden of Alkinoos.

II

The best account in English of the life of St. John of the Cross is Gerald Brenan's *Horizon* article—the first of two—May, 1947, to which the following is largely indebted.

Born in 1542 in a village of Old Castile, Juan de Yepes was brought up in great poverty by a widowed mother. As a youth he worked as carpenter, tailor, painter; he had some training in art and later drew a remarkable crucifixion which Salvador Dali has made famous. He loved music, particularly the popular songs of the people. In school he probably became acquainted with the Latin poets; he would have heard all around him the Spanish *romances* or folk ballads, unrivaled in Europe.

Becoming at twenty-one a Carmelite friar, he spent four years at the University of Salamanca. Biblical studies obviously claimed a good part of his time, since "no protestant divine ever quoted Scripture more often." Just before leaving the university he met Teresa of Avila, then past fifty, and became interested in her project for the reform of the Carmelite order: its return to a more primitive rule that would stress prayer and contemplation. In 1568, as Juan de la Cruz, he took his vows with the Reformed Carmelites. For about the next ten years his existence, in a simple country monastery and as confessor to the convent at Avila, was outwardly uneventful.

Then in 1577 he became the key figure in a cloak-and-dagger episode. Because of the violent hostility of the unreformed Carmelites and a more far-reaching suspicion of Reformed Carmelite practices (St. John himself had been denounced to the Inquisition) he was kidnapped and dragged off to the Priory at Toledo—the large building, now destroyed, to the right of the bridge in El Greco's Plan of Toledo. There he was shut in a gloomy, ill-smelling little closet; half starved; permitted no change of his flea-ridden clothing for eight months, and beaten by his unreformed brethren at frequent intervals with such zeal that his shoulders were crippled for life.

In the midst of his sufferings, he heard one evening from the street below a popular song about unhappy love—sixteenth-century blues:

> *Muérome de amores,*
> *Carillo, qué haré?*
> *—Que te mueras, alahé!*

Always susceptible to the charm of music and poetry, capable of seeing them *a lo divino* (as symbolizing the love between God and man), St. John, enraptured by the sadness and beauty of that worldly song, was himself inspired to expression. His greatest lyrics, the *Cántico* and the *Noche*, and some others were written in whole or in part during these months in prison, precisely *nel mezzo del cammin di nostra vita*.

His escape, the following August, was as melodramatic as the kidnapping eight months earlier. With ropes twisted from strips of blanket and tunic, he let himself down from a dizzy height into the darkness. Somehow, after a stunning fall and mysterious assistance over a wall too high to climb, he found his way, through the blackness of a strange city, to the Reformed Camelite Convent; there he was taken in "looking like an image of death," and given pears stewed with cinnamon. That he regarded his poetry as more than a pastime is shown, the very day of his escape, by his dictating some verses he had composed in prison but had been unable to write down.

The following spring was spent at a mountain hermitage, rugged and beautiful, in Andalusia. Here he completed the lyrics, and his dazzling career as poet, which had opened not many months before, was "practically finished." Then followed three years at Baeza, farther down the Guadalquivír. The charm of landscape, all the forces of nature, were an unfailing inspiration to him—what saves this oldest of clichés is that in him they actually inspired something: praise of God for the beauty of created being and for the knowledge of Him which we derive from it; this he referred to, with great affection, as *the knowledge of the evening*, distinct from the daylight knowledge of God in Himself.

In 1582 he went to Granada as prior for three quiet years; on the hillside not far from the Alhambra, "with one of the most beautiful views in the world before him," he wrote his long commentaries on the poems. In the years that followed, as Vicar General for Andalusia, he traveled widely, by burro, through southern Spain, going even as far as Lisbon and Madrid, sleeping, like Don Quijote, in the open air or in the brawling, overcrowded inns. In 1588, as new dangers threatened in the order, he became prior at Segovia, a post he held until May of 1591, when his insistence on chapter elections by secret ballot led to his disgrace and removal to a solitary spot in Andalusia. To destroy him once and for all, enemies within his own order set about collecting or fabricating evidence. Feeling ran so high that, rather than risk guilt by association, people with letters or papers from him thought it safer to destroy them. Only his final illness saved him from further persecution: in September of 1591 he was brought low with fever and terrible ulcers; these proving uncontrollable, on December 14th of that year he died, his voice rising from the rotted flesh in delight at the beauties of the *Song of Songs*. Almost immediately there were wild public demonstrations in his favor. Popularly recognized as a saint even in his own lifetime, he was canonized in 1726, proclaimed a Doctor of the Church in 1926. There are no specific references to the external events of his life in his poetry, which is surely rich, however, in such reminiscences as Brenan points out in speaking of the last lines of the *Cántico*:

> *Y el cerco sosegaba,*
> *Y la caballería*
> *A vista de las aguas descendía.*

I do not think that in the whole of Spanish poetry there is a passage that calls up so vividly the Castilian-Andalusian scene: the line of horses or mules descending slowly to the river; the vague suggestion of frontier warfare, now over: that sense of endless repetition, of something that has been done countless times before being done again, which is the gift of Spain to the restless and progressive nations. In those last two wonderful lines with their gently reassuring fall, the horses descending within sight of the waters are lifted out of time and made the symbol of the peace of this Heracleitan land of eternal recurrence.

Nowhere in St. John's work or in what we know of his life does he indicate the slightest sense of embarrassment or self-consciousness (or pride) about his poetry, or the slightest regret when he came to write no more. Apparently he had no scruples about its being in conflict with other interests: he urged the religious under him to improvise verses *a lo divino* in their times of recreation. He left it with no grand gestures of renunciation. At times he enjoyed indulging his facility: some of his verses are mere exuberant improvisings. When moved by delight and love to express himself by way of poetry, he did so as no other ever has; when moved by delight and love to pass beyond that stage, he went gayly into *la música callada*. One feels from his writings that no man has ever found a richer wonderland of delight or wasteland of darkness than St. John found in his own soul, often at altitudes quite beyond poetry. Probably during much of his life the intensity of his experience was too great to need or admit of expression. What Yeats has written about the poet and human love here comes to mind: had the poet been successful in love

> who can say
> What would have shaken from the sieve?
> I might have thrown poor words away
> And been content to live.

As indeed St. John was, though "content" is too weak a word, and though his life was not the life his companions—and still less the strangers around him—were able to see.

"There are certain kinds of sanctity," said St. Teresa in one of her marvelously barbed remarks, "I do not understand." These twisted sorts of sanctity would include that of people who turn to religion and "God" out of weak blood or nightmare terrors or *mal protesi nervi* or plain hatred of the world: the feeling that if they had had the making

of it, many loose ends in existence would have been tucked in with
more niceness and propriety. St. John's holiness was far from being
of this sort. He saw everything created as fresh and beautiful; saw,
without Hopkins' torment, "the dearest freshness deep down things."
The fields, the flowers, the animals, men and angels, wine, companion-
ship, poetry, the singing voice—all were beautiful. Most rapturous
of all was human love. He saw the evening world as very good, but
saw beyond it something realler and more thrilling. We fall in love,
we others, with our bright particular star, he with the infinite galaxies
of Night.

III

Poetry, we would all agree with Robert Frost, is what is lost in
translation. In it thought and passion have settled precisely to their
liking in the canebrake of words and have no mind to move: they
rest there, as Dante said of intellect discovering truth, *come fera in
lustra*—like a wild beast in its lair.

A few commonplaces: first, the poem is not its content. If it were,
anyone with a dictionary and neatly lined paper could make his own
translations. I have not settled for putting down the meaning of word
after word, in order as they come—and not only because order in one
language is chaos in another. The meaning of poetry is a concord, or
sometimes a discord, of many elements: of rhythm, of the sound
of words and all it conjures, of the way our lips and throat relax or
struggle to pronounce them, of the way words rebel against or nestle
with each other, of their past record in the language and the company
they have kept, of all their haloes, induced currents, and blue leaping
arcs.

St. John knew very well that poetry, by its own peculiar means
that by-pass logic, can do something that rational discourse despairs
of. Hence the almost apologetic way in which he begins his prose

explications. "The glory of poetry," says Dámaso Alonso, "consists in its being the only way of organizing human speech so that it can somehow approach the mysteries of divinity. The true mystical heights of St. John are not to be found in the commentaries, but in the poems." And not, we must insist, in the "thought" of the poems—which are always closer, says Alonso, to the ineffable experience.

My venture, the windmill I am tilting at, is to give some inkling of the poetry. That means that I have chosen the rhythms and forms of the original instead of turning the content into a slack free verse favorable, perhaps, to thought and imagery, but at what fatal cost to their pulsing blood-rhythms!—rhythms very different from those brain-rhythms that count beads on a wooden abacus. It means too that I have aimed at the kind of diction St. John used: a diction direct and colloquial, sometimes rustic, sometimes solemn with echoes of the *Song of Songs* or the courtly pastoral. And, since "the sound," as Frost has said, "is the gold in the ore," it means I have tried to do something about sound values and special sound effects. When St. John writes,

un no sé qué que quedan balbuciendo

one shirks the true task if he translates "a something they keep stammering." The three *que*'s have embedded the stammer in the very being of the line, with an effect the translator cannot ignore.

Ernest Jones has described how Freud translated: "Instead of laboriously transcribing from the foreign language, idioms and all, he would read a passage, close the book, and consider how a German writer would have clothed the same thoughts—a method not very common among translators." But a highly sensible way: otherwise one merely turns the poor content out of its comfortable home into the dreary winter of no-language.

The translator of poetry has a far more ticklish task: he has to consider not just what to say but how to say it in certain images, rhythms, and sounds. What this amounts to is writing a poem of his own, using as much of the material of the original as he possibly can. His doom is that there will always be parts left over and gaps he will have to caulk with inferior oakum. If he keeps the rhythms of the original he may even find that they have a different relationship to diction in the new language. What does the translator of Dante, for example, do about the fact that many common words which in English have one syllable (boy, girl, day, night, love, hate, birth, death) in Italian have two or more?

The attempt to translate a poem on these principles is drudgery more demanding, if less noble, that writing a poem wholly one's own. None of the fairy-tale injunctions Bellissima lays upon her suitors is as arduous as what the Muse of translation continually demands: "Compose first a seven-syllable line meaning 'Where did you hide,' with two dominant accents reinforced by an identical hollow sound (they must mean *where* and *hide* but sound more like *oar* and *ode*), and with the final syllable being one of the dozen or so words that rime with *art*, and make quite sure that the whole thing is like the heart-broken cry of an abandoned lover—hence no 'hidest' or 'whither' or 'enshrouded' or any of that tinsel or batting—and be quick about it: we have two hundred more lines to get on to!" And the sphinx sits back ready to demand her next squared circle.

The poor translator rarely comes up with anything better than a shabby gadget likely to fly to pieces if held near the magic original. If the solutions only had a logic as fairy as the demands, a hook in the nearest pool would produce a fish with the phrase like a golden ring in its mouth—but the problems the sphinx proposes raving have to be solved in the cold light of day with whatever resources the work-man has at hand.

"*A dónde te escondiste. . . ?*" How simple, and how untranslatable. "Where did you hide. . . ?" But the effect of the wonderful line, written in the stone loneliness of the prison, is in the very reverberance of *dond* and *cond*; and the dwindling echo of *de te, diste*. The English words *where* and *hide* have not a sound in common for the echo; what sounds they have are flat, thin, without timbre. In English the life has gone out of the line. For many years now, haunted by those hollow sounds, I have tried the line a hundred ways.

Nothing has squared the circle.

THE SPANISH TEXT

Although such distinguished editions as those of P. Gerardo (1912–1914) and P. Silverio (1929–1931) have gone far toward arriving at an authoritative text of St. John of the Cross, Dámaso Alonso was still able, in 1946, to make a strong plea for the *"verdadera—e indispensable—edición científica."* The edition of the Biblioteca de Autores Cristianos (Madrid, 1950) does not claim final validity: it admits that with the possibility of new codices turning up "one cannot yet declare any text definitive."

For present purposes, it seems desirable to offer a Spanish text as close as possible to what the poet actually wrote, one that will show as little as possible the well-intentioned but sometimes meddling editorial hand—the more so as no text so virgin has yet been presented along with an English translation.

These assumptions pointed clearly to the text at present *más autorizado* according to Dámaso Alonso and *de indiscutible autoridad* for the B.A.C. editors: the text of the Codex of Sanlúcar de Barrameda, preserved in the Carmelite convent of the town of that name near Cadiz. It contains the *Cántico espiritual* and the principal poems, apparently transcribed by a careful and devoted hand. What gives the manuscript its supreme value is the fact that St. John himself (authorities almost without exception agree) examined it *"con cariño"*—read it through, corrected errors, made notes and additions in his own hand—in short, proofread it—many years before the poems were published. All this not only guarantees the authenticity of the text but provides an irresistible emotional appeal: we are seeing the very text the poet saw and approved.

If there is any disadvantage in using sixteenth-century Spanish instead of the modernizations we are familiar with, the fascination of the codex more than countervails the initial difficulty, which in any case is slight. This, after all, is the way we are used to seeing— and indeed insist on seeing—such writers as Jonson, Donne, and Webster, roughly St. John's contemporaries, in sound modern editions.

In Part I, then, I follow the Codex of Sanlúcar for the poems it contains. The text of the four poems of Part II and the Jaén redaction of the *Cántico* (Part III) follow the standard edition of P. Silverio de Santa Teresa.

THE CODEX OF SANLÚCAR DE BARRAMEDA:

PRESENT EDITION

The Codex of Sanlúcar de Barrameda was published in an *edición fototipográfica* (as *Cántico espiritual y poesías de San Juan de la Cruz*) edited by P. Silverio de Santa Teresa, C.D., Tipografía El Monte Carmelo, Burgos, 1928. The two-volume edition reproduces the codex on the left-hand pages, prints the text on the right. It contains the *Cántico espiritual* (poem and prose explication), and, following this, "*las principales poesías que conocemos del Santo.*" The transcription in the Spanish edition exactly follows the manuscript, we are told; if there have been any slips they can easily be corrected by looking across the page (*Si algún desliz se ha escapado, es fácil de subsanar por la reproducción fotográfica*). As a matter of fact the transcribers have not been over-careful: there are at least forty errors, mostly trivial, in the text of the poems alone. When there has been a discrepancy between the photographed manuscript and the transcription, I have followed the manuscript.

This does not aspire to be a scholarly edition of the codex; it aims merely at transferring the text of the poems soundly and clearly to the printed page. I have first of all corrected the errors of the printed transcription, some of which are apparently misprints (*estale y*) for *esta ley*, etc.) and most of which are unimportant misreadings or modernizings of the manuscript. Besides these misreadings, the transcriber sometimes takes for an acute accent the slash or hook which is written, apparently at random, over many *i*'s, especially in the termination of the imperfect tense. I find no basis for this in the manuscript; these slashes are used indifferently over *i*'s that would or would not have the written accent today.

I have put each new poem on a new page, rather than follow the pagination of the manuscript, which begins a new poem directly at the close of the preceding one. Changing the pagination, I have omitted the catchwords occasionally used. In the ballads, a capital letter is used eight times at the beginning of a line only because it is the first line on its page: these now otiose capitals have been removed. The symbol *q̄*, used half a dozen times, in lengthened to *que*; the appropriate nasal is added to three or four *ū*'s. Five or six times a period or other mark clearly mistaken or misleading is removed—a period, for example, in what can only be the middle of a sentence. About a dozen flamboyant capitals (all *A*'s or *D*'s) in midsentence have been humbled. In the twelfth stanza of the *Cántico*, where there is a change of speaker, I have transferred to the margin the speech-prefix, which had been written in, above midline, as a correction, and divided the stanza between the speakers. In the twenty-eighth stanza I have corrected the erroneous *su* to *tu*, which is correctly given twice when the line is quoted in the prose explication. (In the codex the poem is written out in full; then each stanza is quoted separately for explication; under the stanza-explications individual lines are quoted. When the text differs, I follow the text of the poem given in full, with the exception just mentioned.) I have bestowed a cedilla on the *c* of *disfraçada* in the *Noche oscura*, and corrected the irregular indentations of the third stanza of that poem. Otherwise the text printed here gives exactly what the author himself let stand.

ORTHOGRAPHY

The sixteenth-century orthography of the Sanlúcar codex is not more remote than that of English texts of the period. Though words are not necessarily spelled the same even when repeated in the same line, spelling is far more regular than English spelling contemporary with it. There were almost no written accents; punctuation was much lighter than today. The Sanlúcar pages are pleasantly clean and uncluttered when compared with those of modern editions, fairly bristling with all kinds of pointers nudging and nagging at the text.

Y and *i*, *u* and *v* may change about, just as in these lines attributed to Raleigh:

> To serue, to liue, to looke vpon those eies,
> To looke, to liue, to kisse that heauenlie hand . . .

So we find *ymagen*, *yguale*, *deleyte*, *posseŷa*, *oyr*, *yre* (*iré*), *yrelo*, etc.; on the other hand *y* ("and") is sometimes written *i*. We find *vivo* or *uiuo*, *ver* or *uer*, *va* or *ua*, *aves* or *aues*. The *u-v* interchange is complicated by the fact that in the Spanish *v* and *b* stand for the same sound ("*ningún puro castellano sabe hazer diferencia*," it was observed in 1558). Modern *enviar* may appear as *embiar* or *enbiar*; *vivir* as *biuir*, *volvería* as *bolueria*, *vuelo* as *buelo*, *volar* as *bolar*, etc. *B* may also appear as *u*: the imperfect ending is commonly written *-aua* instead of *-aba*, though in one long series of imperfects the Sanlúcar text uses both forms. We find *auer* for *haber*, *aura* for *habrá*, *auia* for *había*, *auiendome* for *habiéndome*, *beui* for *bebí*, *caualleria* for *caballería*, *siluo* for *silbo*, *trauajo* for *trabajo*, etc.

J and *x* had the same sound and were used interchangeably: *baxo*, *debaxo*, *exercicio*, *exido*, *dixe*, *dexar*, *dexo* (*dejó*), *dexame* (*déjame*), *dexeme* (*dejéme*), etc.

Z is found where today we are used to *c*, as in *hazer* (*haziendo*, *hize*, etc.), and *dezir* (*dize*, *dezia*, *dezilde*, etc.). *Z* (or *c*) may appear as *ç*: *braço*, *mançano*, *coraçon*, *esperança*, *caça*, *lançe*, etc.

The familiar *h* is missing in *oy*, *e*, *a*, etc. But *eran* is found as *heran*.

G is found for *j* in *ageno*, *trages*, *mensagero*, etc.

Qu is found for *cu* in *quan* (*cuán*), *quando*, *quanto*, *qual*, *enquentro*, etc.

Some letters are doubled: *assi* (*así*), *desseo*, *esso*, *fee*, *passe* (*pasé*), *passo* (*pasó*), *posseo*, etc. Or the reverse: *arabales*, *ariba*, *deramando*, etc.

Some words now combined were left separate: *entrado se* (*entrádose*), *a le* (*hale*), *de el*, etc. Or the reverse: *ençelada*, *acabo*, *della*, *dellos*, *desta*, etc.

A few old or familiar forms are used: *comigo* (*conmigo*), *contino* (*continuo*), *mesmo* (*mismo*), *muncho* (*mucho*), *Sant* (*San*). A few other forms no longer current will be readily recognized: *Christo*, *gerarchia* (*jerarquía*), *nymphas*, *prosteros* (*postreros*), *thalamo* (*tálamo*).

NOTES ON THE POEMS

The following notes are frequently indebted to:

PSJ   Dámaso Alonso, *La Poesía de San Juan de la Cruz*. Madrid, 1946.

PE   *Poesía española, ensayo de métodos y límites estilísticos*. Madrid, 1950.

Gerald Brenan,   "St. John of the Cross: His Life and Poetry." *Horizon* (London). May, June 1947.

LSP   *The Literature of the Spanish People*. Cambridge, 1953.

The Spiritual Canticle (pp. 2–17)

Much of the poem was written during St. John's painful imprisonment at Toledo in 1578: the influence of that harsh environment has been felt in the powerful reverberations of the opening lines. In prison the poet wrote as far as the stanza beginning *"O ninfas de Judea"*— the reference is probably to the stanzaic order of the first version. Of the remaining stanzas, all but the last five were written, not long after his escape, at Baeza—"one likes to think . . . by the banks of the Guadalimar, in the woods of the Granja de Santa Ana" (P. Silverio-Peers). The last five stanzas were written at Granada (where he resided from 1582 to 1585) under the influence of an access of delight and love he felt to hear a nun report that her prayers were given to "considering the beauty of God and . . . rejoicing that he has such beauty."

St. John of the Cross, though he felt that poetry gave fuller expression to (or richer intimations of) his experiences than prose exposition could hope to (the latter can give only "the least part of that which they contain") was prevailed on to write a prose explication of the poem, stanza-by-stanza, line-by-line. Probably while examining the poem—itself all élan and ardor—with the critic's eye, he decided that a rearrangement of many of the stanzas would bring them in closer correspondence with the mystical progress he was describing. The result is the "second redaction" or "new Spiritual Canticle" of the Codex of Jaén (cf. pp. 98–115 and the notes to those pages). Although the second version may be more satisfactory to the student of mystical theology, the first has long been recognized as the finer poem. For a study in English of the two versions, cf. I. I. Macdonald, "The Two Versions of the *Cántico Espiritual*," Mod. Lang. Notes, XXV, pp. 165–184 (April, 1930).

Echoes of St. John's favorite poetry, that of the *Song of Songs*, are of course everywhere in the "Canticle," which is indebted also to Garcilaso (and through him to Italian Renaissance poetry) for some features of the pastoral treatment, for the hendecasyllabic rhythm of the long lines, and for the stanza known as the *lira* (used also in "The Dark Night")—a form devised by Bernardo Tasso to suggest Horatian effects in a stressed language. The *lira* was used also by Fray Luis de Leon, who lectured at Salamanca during the years St. John of the Cross was there. The peculiar feature of this combination of seven- and eleven-syllable lines consists in "the way in which the last long line of each stanza, coming as it does after two short ones, the second of which rhymes with it, rolls forward like the fringe of a wave to reach a new high-water mark." (Brenan, LSP, pp. 157–8.)

The general impression of the "Spiritual Canticle" has been eloquently described by Gerald Brenan in the second of his *Horizon* articles:

> "The *Cántico* starts with a cry of longing and anguish, but almost at once this changes to an air-borne feeling of lightness, clarity, exhilaration, speed of movement. There is a sense of travel and adventure: mountains, rivers, valleys, dawns, breezes, ' strange islands ' come and go: lions, antelopes, birds, flowers are seen and left behind. There are gusts of passion and tenderness and then the clear Castilian air grows

heavy for a moment with the scent of cedar wood and lilies, whilst the lovers, in walled gardens or rocky caves or on castle battlements, meet together to perform their mysterious rites. Yet the voluptuousness which blows in from the East is tempered to an astonishing delicacy. This poetry is virginal; and there is at times a penetrating strangeness of tone that recalls—as very little poetry really recalls—the pathos of dreams."

The Dark Night (pp. 18–21)

Said, though without positive evidence, to have been written in prison; written, at any rate, not long after. For Jean Baruzi (*Saint Jean de la Croix et le problème de l'expérience mystique*) the night-symbolism of this poem (and the following one) constitutes St. John's most original and profound intuition. The influence of Arabic mysticism here and elsewhere has been suggested but not established. To expound the poem ("each stanza . . . and the lines of each stanza") St. John wrote "The Ascent of Mount Carmel" and "The Dark Night of the Soul." Both are incomplete; nearly 500 pages of explication cover little more than the first ten lines of the poem. For a recent study, cf. Leo Spitzer, "Three Poems on Ecstasy (John Donne, St. John of the Cross, Richard Wagner)" in *A Method of Interpreting Literature*.

The Living Flame of Love (pp. 22–23)

This poem belongs to the Granada period, probably to 1583 or 1584. The poet has himself explained the stanzaic structure in a famous note near the beginning of the prose explication of this poem: "The structure of these *liras* are [sic] like those which in Boscán are given a divine meaning [he quotes three lines] and in which there are six lines, the fourth riming with the first, the fifth with the second, and the sixth with the third." Alonso (PE, pp. 287–9) analyzes this curious note, with its uncorrected syntax, its reference to the joint *Obras de Boscán y Garcilaso* simply as "*Boscán*" and the reference to *liras*— actually the stanza form he uses is the first half of a complicated *canción* stanza of Garcilaso. The lines quoted are not from the original, but from the pious revision of Sebastián de Córdoba, who rewrote

Garcilaso *a lo divino*. Alonso (PSJ, p. 146) thinks the lamps of the third stanza—which he considers one of the poet's most concentrated and significant images—were suggested by a phrase of the *Song of Songs*: "lampades ejus, lampades ignis atque flammarum."

In the last line of stanza 2, most editors have preferred the comma after *matando* rather than after *muerte*.

Deep Rapture (pp. 24–29)

A *villancico* of the familiar Castilian type. Typically a popular dance-song, the *villancico* develops an initial theme of from two to four lines (the *estribillo*) in stanzas that end with a line or two of the theme. Alonso suspects that the theme (often borrowed or traditional) was in this case invented by the poet. Basic in the thought of St. John (and one does not have to read far in the poet to agree with Alonso in this) is this juxtaposition of opposites, this recourse to contraries in the struggle against the limitations of human speech. In the decade between PSJ and PE Alonso's admiration for this poem increased from "a masterpiece in a minor key" to "nothing less than one of the best definitions of our national *irracionalidad*, and one of the peaks of the whole range of Spanish poetry." The phrase *"no entender entendiendo"* is from the work of St. Teresa.

Life No Life (pp. 30–35)

This poem, like the preceding one, develops, with refrain, an initial theme—glossed also by St. Teresa. Versions attributed to her contain some stanzas apparently interpolated from the text of St. John. The paradoxical life-death theme, which flourished in courtly tradition back at least to the troubadours, is of course a universal commonplace, from Euripides' queries about life-as-death and death-as-life (in fragments from the lost *Polyidus* and *Phrixus*) to T. S. Eliot's "death by water" and "hour of our birth."

Of Falconry (pp. 36–39)

A long line of Spanish poems had seen the course of human love and its pursuit in falconry images; some of these *a lo divino*. This poem of St. John was suggested by a rather poor anonymous verse evidently about human love: St. John has taken for his theme the first four lines of the older poem with the change of only a word or two and developed them independently. The pursuit is referred to only in general terms in the Spanish: those familiar with the sport and the poetic tradition would understand that the quarry was the heron (as it is, explicitly, in many of the falconry poems): I have specified both birds in the translation. Hawking for the heron was regarded as perhaps the noblest and most thrilling form of the sport: the heron, with its large wings and light body, could rise in sheer, almost perpendicular rings, and when alarmed would make for the upper air; the falcon, in wide, sweeping circles because of its greater weight, strength, and speed, would gradually overtake the heron, perhaps in the very clouds, soaring high above to dive for the quarry.

Madrigal (pp. 40–41)

This poignant and melancholy poem, which Brenan finds "the tenderest of his *canciones*" cannot be dated precisely but would seem to be early, conceivably belonging even to a period before the imprisonment. Without the rhythmic velocity of the greater poems, this has the feeling of a pastoral piece by Garcilaso *a lo divino*—it is more than likely, in fact, that the device of shepherd-and-tree was suggested by its use in Sebastián de Córdoba's versions. Alonso points out that in some ways this poem resembles the anonymous fifteenth-century English *Quia Amore Langueo*. The source has only recently been found by José Blecua in the Bibliothèque Nationale. At first glance it would seem that St. John had followed his source quite closely; actually his remodeling of the material has been subtle and expressive.

It is analyzed by Alonso (PE, pp. 284–6) who sees, in St. John's disregard for the regularity of the original, evidence of his unconcern for technique and formal perfection: Alonso roundly declares that not a single great poet of the sixteenth or seventeenth centuries— indeed, not a single competent rimester!—could have proceeded so:

others would either have kept the regularity of the original or, if they departed, made a pattern of the departure. But can one be so sure St. John's procedure indicates unconcern? Or merely a superior sense of form that was not content to balance external devices? The practice of some of the best English poets might lead us to suspect the latter.

Song of the Soul (pp. 42–45)

These *coplas* were said to have been composed in prison. Alonso finds the poem strange in every way: he thinks the form *fonte* (instead of the normal *fuente*) of the first line indicates an ancient dialectal assonance with the *noche* of the short line—from this he concludes that the original form of the *villancico* had three short lines instead of a long line and a short line. Probably, he suggests, St. John was developing an old *villancico* from the west, now lost—but developing it, most strangely of all, not in the rhythms of folk poetry but in that fashionable and highbrow importation, the Italian hendecasyllable. For further peculiarities, cf. PSJ, p. 118 and *passim*. Brenan finds this "disturbing" poem "one of the most original and beautiful"; he sees in it a highly independent handling of the *villancico*: St. John "has taken, as the custom was, his *estribillo* from an old popular song, altering it perhaps a little; then he has shortened the stanzas to two lines each and let the weight of the poem rest on the peculiarly insinuating refrain, which acts on the reader with the effect of a whispered incantation." The symbolism of flowing water, PSJ reminds us, was common in the mystics: certain Franciscan writers used for the Trinity the triple symbol of fountain, river, and sea.

Ballads (pp. 46–81)

The group of nine ballads, and the ballad that follows on the psalm *Super flumina Babylonis*, were composed in prison. Some at least were dictated by St. John from memory, immediately after his escape, to one of the nuns who gave him shelter—they were described then as "so sublime and devout that they seemed to enkindle the reader."

But these poems on theological themes, in the rhythms and language of the popular ballads (the same rime in *ia* is carried relentlessly through all nine) have not often come in for such praise: they are likely to be thought of as among the poet's more perfunctory pieces. Yet Dámaso Alonso, himself a poet of distinction, speaks up for them: he declares that in their very rusticity and sameness they have a certain transparency, a tangy freshness or harsh charm.

Without and With Mainstay (pp. 84–87)

Neither this poem nor the one that follows is found in the Sanlúcar codex or the first published edition of the poems. Though included in the Codex of Jaén, their attribution to St. John of the Cross is not beyond question. For this poem, no definite model has been found; it seems probably enough that both theme and development were inventions of the author.

The Hunter's Quest (pp. 88–93)

Cf. comment on the preceding poem. *The Hunter's Quest* is based on a poem published in 1580 with an almost identical initial theme: a poem that refers, with a certain ambiguity, to idealized human love. The author, Pedro de Padilla, five years later himself became a Carmelite. St. John (if he is the author) develops de Padilla's theme *a lo divino*.

Divine Word (pp. 94–95)

Alonso finds no irrefragable evidence for the authenticity of either of the little verses on these pages. St. John is reported to have urged the religious under his direction to compose, during times of recreation, verses that would enkindle divine love. *Divine Word* is said to have been improvised by the saint for a Christmas celebration in the monastery of Granada when he was prior there.

The Capsule of Perfection (pp. 94–95)

Attributed to St. John by P. Esteban de San José in 1667.

The Spiritual Canticle (Revised Version) (pp. 98–115)

Cf. the Notes to "The Spiritual Canticle" (pp. 2–17). In the revised version, which appears in the Codex of Jaén, the eleventh stanza ("Appear here at my side . . .") is added; otherwise both versions are the same up to the beginning of the sixteenth stanza ("Now that the bloom uncloses . . ."). The last seven stanzas are in the same order in both versions. Stanzas in between are altered in the interests of a more logical and systematic account of the progress from the state of Spiritual Betrothal to the loftier state of Spiritual Marriage. In the first version, fifteen stanzas are concerned with the Betrothal of the soul to God (from the first appearance of the Bridegroom in the twelfth stanza to the twenty-seventh stanza, which begins "She enters, the bride!"). In the second version, only five stanzas, beginning at the same point as in the first version, are given to this stage. The other ten, from the fifteenth ("Our bed: in roses laid . . .") to the twenty-fourth ("Please, no pitying brow . . .") have been transferred to the state of Spiritual Marriage, since they refer to a security of bliss apparently thought beyond the capacities of the earlier state. Four stanzas of the first version which describe misgivings of the soul in the state of Spiritual Marriage ("Girls of Jerusalem . . . islands in her chase . . ." "Wings twinkling here and there . . . deep slumber fall") are transferred to the lower state, more likely to be troubled by such apprehensions. This is all to the good, since as P. Silverio has said it leaves the two states "much more precisely differentiated and clearly described." But these schematic gains have perhaps been achieved at too great a cost. These Notes are not the place for a through study of the two versions—but readers will surely notice that though in theory the continuity of the revision is better, in the fact of the poem it sometimes falters. In the revised version, for example, the little foxes and the chilling wind are brought in too abruptly after the ecstasy of the preceding stanzas, and the entrance of the bride into the garden (the twenty-second stanza) is not only less dramatic (since in mid-speech) but even anticlimactic, since she has been described as sleeping securely in the stanza before. The apparent inconsistencies of the first version can even be defended: the too great happiness of the Betrothed (the mention of the flowery bed, for example) can be seen as anticipations, visions, longings—the garden, when she does finally enter it, is described as *deseado* ("longed for"). The apprehensive stanzas in the first account of the Spiritual Marriage can be explained on the grounds that in the poem itself they sound by no means so ominous as the explications would have them; and in any event the Spiritual Marriage is attainable in this life, and hence is not a condition of unshakable security.